BEV!

The Invisible Sister

Rory Janis Miller

PINE TOP PRESS
Bethlehem, PA

Bev: to PH - asc 9
our - 41.
died - 2015

1943 - 2015 = 72

° 3 eras 9
Bev's b/a

ISBN-13: 978-0692645185 (Pine Top Press)

ISBN-10: 0692645187

Rory Miller Maruschak: Bethlehem, Pennsylvania 18017

Ac-

PINE TOP PRESS
Bethlehem, PA

knowledgments

My sister Bev has taken me on an amazing journey filled with revelation and serendipity. It all started with a group of women called Les Amis who, in giving me the pleasure of writing down their unique history, planted the seeds of my own memoir. Although this book started out as a mere collection of family memories, once I discovered Bev's Pennhurst records it became so much more. If it hadn't been for Carol Hillard, who told me that those records existed and where I could find them, that would never had happened. Then it was Kathy O'Rourke Rees, who not only helped me access those records but also added to them by recounting some of her own experiences at Pennhurst. Still, the most important element of the story is family. I want to thank my brother Greg and my sister Jonnie for adding their memories to my own and for helping me sort them all out. Of course, special thanks must go to my husband Greg, the indefatigable chauffeur, who makes sure I always get there.

After years of morphing, this story would never have been ready to meet the public without the expertise of my wonderful editor Andrea Sizemore. From early drafts to the finished product, she provided not only her editing skill, but also encouragement and loving support along the way. Thanks to the Greater Lehigh Valley Writers Group, I found the guy to put the whole project together. My gratitude goes to Bart Palamaro at Dark Horse Productions for not only his technical expertise, but also his advice and wisdom. For the amazing cover design I thank Hannah Ehret for the artistic vision that captured the essence of the story so beautifully.

Inside the book, though most of the photos came from my family album, the images of Pennhurst were generously provided by J. Gregory Pirmann from his book *Pennhurst State School and Hospital*. I also thank Greg for taking the time to read the final manuscript and for making his invaluable observations and corrections. I would like to thank author Karl Williams, both for sharing his advice and for graciously giving his permission to use quoted lines from his book with Roland Johnson, *Lost in a Desert World*.

As *Bev* neared completion, I was very fortunate to get to know Rachel Simon, author of *Riding the Bus with My Sister*, a book which inspired me as I wrote about my relationship with my own sister. I thank her for taking the time out from her busy schedule to read my manuscript, and I am grateful for all of our conversations, which she has filled with insight, wisdom, and empathy. Rachel, Karl, and Greg have all embraced Bev's story and have given me the courage to believe in myself as a writer who could put her life into words. I would also like to thank all the good people at Threshold Rehabilitation Services and SAM for their devotion to Bev and for their desire to see her story told.

And last but never least, I thank Charlotte, my dear friend and writer extraordinaire, who would have been so proud.

Author's Note

I feel that I should make a comment about some of the terminology used in my story. Some of the words that appear may seem offensive in light of today's social awareness. The words that I used were the terms that I grew up with and that were in general use during the time frame of this story. They are also the words that appeared in many of the letters, documents, and reports that I read while doing my research. Today those terms are no longer considered appropriate. I have changed the terminology whenever I felt I could, but much of it is left in place in its historical context.

For my mother and father

All sorrows can be borne if we put them in a story or tell a story about them.

Isak Dinesen

Contents

PREFACE

There is a photograph on the shelf above my computer, part of a small gallery of family pictures that watch over me while I work. It is an 8x10 professional portrait in sepia tones showing six people, my family as they were late in the year of 1951 or early 1952. It is unique, the only such portrait we ever had taken. We all look very stiff, very posed, very serious.

On the far left of the photo is my mother Amelia, holding my baby sister Jonnie, around 14 months old, on her lap. Mother is wearing a suit, the jacket buttoned up the front to the neck. Although the sepia tones show no color, I remember vividly the colors of everyone's clothing. That suit jacket was light brown with brown and tan and coral colored piping that matched a checkered skirt with the same pattern. Little Jonnie, in a blue plaid dress with a white collar, is happily playing with the laces of her scuffed white shoes. On the far right stands my father John, dressed in a camel colored corduroy jacket with wide lapels, a dark sweater vest and a bow tie. Standing between our parents is my nine and a half year old brother Greg, wearing a red plaid shirt and a navy jacket that he had yet to grow into. Seated in front of Greg is myself, a bit past 4 years old. I am wearing a light blue short sleeved dress with two red plaid stripes across the bodice and two above the hem. Sitting next to me, and in front of my father, is Beverley, age 8 1/2. She has on a brown and white hounds tooth patterned dress with a large round collar and three quarter length sleeves, a dress I remember wearing years later as a hand-me-down.

Beverley is a beautiful child with dark brown hair, dark eyes under straight bangs, and a distant dreamy expression. She looks angelic with her hands folded obediently in her lap. Not long after this photograph was taken, that little girl entered an institution called the Pennhurst State School, and our family lost her forever.

This book is the story of my intellectually disabled sister Beverley. I can tell her story only through my own memories. I explain how her experience affected me and our family, how my thoughts and feelings about what I witnessed haunt me to this day. Piecing the story together hasn't been easy. Our mother, who was never forthcoming with information about Bev, had a way of suppressing many memories, especially the painful ones. When pressed for facts she invariably said she just couldn't remember. Sometimes she truly couldn't remember, but sometimes she simply didn't want to discuss it. Now she is gone, our father is gone, and so are the few other relatives who could have supplied information. The only person who knows the whole story is Bev, and her memories are locked away in her mind just as she herself was once locked away in an institution. Luckily, a wall of medication keeps the nightmares contained - most of the time. I am happy for her oblivion. And so I tell the tale as remembered by myself, with help from my younger sister, Jonnie and older brother, Greg. To our memories I have added facts gleaned from Beverley's Pennhurst records and other documents, as well as additional material from books, Internet sources, and interviews. The story that emerged is a puzzle whose pieces don't always fit, with some pieces missing, with no final solution. One of Bev's favorite activities, and one she is very good at, is putting puzzles together. What a pity she couldn't help me do this one.

When I set out to unravel the puzzle of my sister, I had very little information to go on. My parents and other relatives who would know about Bev's past are all dead. When Greg, Jonnie, and I got together to compare our memories, we realized that we knew very little about our parents and even less about our sister. To make matters worse, my father could tell a lie with the best of them, which always made it hard to know what the truth really was. For all of those reasons, much of our family history remains shrouded in mystery.

When it came to Bev, both our parents avoided talking about her in any detail. Though we knew that she became a resident of the Pennhurst State School and Hospital in southeastern Pennsylvania, we had only the vaguest idea of how or why that happened. Luckily for me, there were records from Pennhurst stored at the Norristown State Hospital that provided me with a great deal of information about Bev's case history. It was from those records that I pieced together my mother's journey through hospitals and doctors' offices in her quest to get help for her daughter. Once Bev was admitted to the Pennhurst State School, those same records documented much of her experience in the institution. Getting at these records wasn't easy. They were stored in a musty old building and made available only through the generous efforts of two staff members who were willing to work in the building for one day every few months so that family members or approved researchers could come in and pore through the stacks of documents. The state hospital bureaucracy seemed to make it as inconvenient as possible for anyone to find or use those records. Indeed, their contents were not for the faint of heart.

I spent many uncomfortable hours in that depressing, derelict old building sifting through hundreds of pages of letters and reports and ledgers documenting my sister's official life history. Most of the story about what happened clinically with Bev in those very early years is contained in copies of four reports dating from October 1951 to February 1952. These brief reports shed some light on Bev's diagnosis and track the efforts Mother made to find help for her within the medical system, from her first encounter with mental health professionals to her eventual admission to the Pennhurst State School. These documents are a puzzle in themselves and contain many discrepancies that give an unclear picture of Bev's mental condition.

I've tried to piece together Bev's confusing journey through a maze of physical exams and psychological tests, but in those days record keeping was not what it is today. The information is poorly arranged and typographical errors abound. It was also disturbing to discover that opinions often seemed to carry more weight than facts. By today's standards these reports seem rambling and disorganized, very unprofessional, yet the people who wrote them were respected members of the mental health community. When I read the reports I have to wonder why the people involved made the decisions they did concerning Bev's treatment. In the cold light of 20/20 hindsight, these haphazardly typed reports are a sad testimony to an antiquated mental health system that failed Bev and so many others like her.

BOOK ONE

1943 - 1952

The First Night

Nine-year-old Beverley lies awake in her bed listening to the thumping of her heart, not quite loud enough to drown out the strange night sounds around her. Last night she slept at home in her own bed, her little sister breathing softly in the bunk above her, her big brother close by, and her parents below her in their bedroom downstairs with the baby. Tonight she is sleeping in a dormitory full of unfamiliar children, snoring and grunting and sniffling around her in the darkness. After being fed and bathed, she was put to bed by strangers in a strange land. She had fussed and cried and pleaded for her mother, to no avail. She is alone, lost in a clinical wilderness. Her fear paralyzes her. It is hard enough to think clearly at the best of times, but tonight her mind is a white wall of blind panic. She does not know what has happened to her. She cannot know that she has been committed to an institution, that this night is just the first step of a journey into insanity, that what she had suffered in her soul before is nothing compared to what is to come, that thirty two years of nights far worse than this lay ahead of her, that hell is a place and she is in it. The name of that place is Pennhurst State School, Spring City, Pennsylvania.

~1~

The Journey Begins

Monday's child is fair of face, Tuesday's child is full of grace, Wednesday's child is full of woe...   Traditional Children's Folk Rhyme

When our parents ran away to Elkton, Maryland to get married, Mother was already pregnant with my brother Greg. Seven month pregnancies were not uncommon in those days. They had no intention of returning home after the clandestine civil ceremony, but fate brought them back for a funeral when one of Mother's sisters passed away. They stayed, and it wasn't long before they settled down in their own little house with their new baby son. Just a year later, they prepared for the birth of their second child. This time it would be different. They were married, they had a house, Dad had a good job. As it turned out, it was very different, indeed.

She was born on a rainy Wednesday, June 9, 1943, a gloomy Pennsylvania day with low hanging clouds and a spring chill in the air. She was their second child, an adorable girl with a full head of straight black hair, and they gave her the name Beverley Lynne. Though she arrived full term after an uneventful pregnancy, what should have been a normal delivery somehow went wrong. Our mother was not sure about what happened, but she told us that her regular obstetrician was not there, that an intern delivered the baby, that the baby came quickly and that no one was prepared. She firmly believed this intern injured her baby when he used forceps to assist the delivery. However it happened, somehow damage occurred to Beverley's brain, either at birth or shortly thereafter, and their beautiful newborn daughter did not develop normally.

I don't know exactly when our mother first realized that Beverley wasn't developing normally or when signs of trouble first appeared. Eventually it became apparent that Bev was on her own timeline for sitting up, crawling, walking, and talking, progressing more slowly than most children. She took longer to reach each milestone and struggled to get there. Mother never discussed these things with us in any detail. When questioned, she gave only the briefest answers and always claimed not to remember the particulars. Nevertheless, she already had one healthy baby, a boy exactly one year older than Bev. Even though Mother was young and relatively inexperienced, she must have been aware of the obvious contrast between Bev and her older brother Greg. The truth couldn't be ignored, and it wouldn't be long before our parents understood the frightening fact that Bev was going to present them with a formidable challenge. For these naive young people, that challenge would become overwhelming. Her birth was the beginning of a long journey which would take them to places no parent should ever have to go.

When Bev was born our parents had been married less than two years and were struggling to make ends meet during the Second World War. Life was tough for everyone. Typical of many couples in those days, our parents married young - our mother nineteen, our father twenty. Most women didn't have careers, they had families. Years later I asked Mom one of those kid questions, "Why do people get married?" "They get married to have children," she said. "Can't people have children if they're not married?" She didn't have an answer ready for that one. I spent my preteen life thinking that once you marched down the aisle God somehow knew you were married and sent you some kids. It was a rude awakening when I found out otherwise.

Our own parents never actually marched down the aisle. They were wed by a justice of the peace in November of 1941, just two weeks before the attack on Pearl Harbor and the entry of the United States into World War II. Although he was drafted, our father somehow managed to fail the service requirements and never enlisted in the army, fulfilling his duty by working in an aircraft factory instead. It was not an auspicious time to start a family, especially when their marriage had already gotten off to a shaky start. My grandmother refused to give her permission for Mother to marry Dad, forcing them to elope to Maryland and marry in secret. Because Mother was already pregnant, they had no time to wait for Granny to change her mind. They were a mismatched couple in so many ways, and the differences between them did not make for an easy road when the going got rough and important decisions needed to be made. They both brought emotional baggage with them that prevented them from building the kind of strong foundation in their relationship that would help them cope later with the demands of raising a family.

Our mother, Amelia, was born in 1922 into a family of Polish immigrants in Hadley, Massachusetts. When she was very young her family moved to Reading, Pennsylvania and settled into a corner row house in a Polish neighborhood. The house sat on a steep hillside street across from a cemetery where Mother would one day bury her fourth child. She had two older sisters and a much younger brother. When she was around twelve years old, her father died from tuberculosis, leaving her mother to take care of four children on her own. Polish was Mother's first language at home, in their neighborhood, and at her Polish Catholic grammar school, and it wasn't until she attended Reading High School that she entered an English speaking world. Our grandmother ran a corner grocery store in the front of their house, one room crammed with the necessities of life, from milk and bread and deli meats to ice cream and penny candy. During the Great Depression of the 1930's, she not only supported her own family, but also kept the neighborhood fed by extending credit and running tabs, many of which were never paid. Though Granny was tough in many ways, she had a soft heart that the neighbors were all too willing to take advantage of. Life was difficult for her and her children during the Depression, but thanks to the store, there was always food on the table and a roof over their heads. Everyone needed to work hard, and Mother and her sisters spent endless hours waiting on customers, doing household chores, and taking care of their little brother, Joe.

After high school, Mother's two older sisters, Mary and Anna, were lucky enough to be able to attend Kutztown State Teacher's College, a small rural college not far from Reading. While her two older sisters were away studying at school, Mother was needed at home to help out in the store as well as to care for her young brother, who was sickly and in and out of the hospital often as a boy. However, only one of her sisters ever graduated from college. Anna, who became ill with tuberculosis and passed away, never had a chance to finish school. Mary did graduate, but instead of using her college degree, she went on to study cosmetology and opened her own beauty shop in Reading. After Mary opened the hair salon, Mother also went to hairdressing school so that she could work with her sister in her shop. So it was that our mother, highly intelligent and academic, wound up toiling away in her sister's beauty salon and in our grandmother's grocery store instead of going to college.

Disappointed that she never got her chance at college and resentful of the fact that she was relegated to a life of drudgery instead of opportunity, Mother wanted desperately to escape and become independent. She was beautiful, intelligent, and full of life. At the same time, she was naive and immature and emotionally vulnerable. When a handsome young man named Johnny Miller pursued her until he swept her off her feet, she fell in love and dreamed of a chance for a new life. If college and a career were not in the picture, she hoped that marriage and her own home and family could help make her feel fulfilled. When she married our father and gave birth to her first baby much too soon thereafter, our grandmother was furious. Her daughter had gone off and married a brash, fast talking rogue instead of a good solid Polish Catholic boy like her older sister had.

Since her family was dead set against her choice of husband, she had to settle for a hasty elopement instead of a proper Catholic wedding. To his credit, Dad did try to win Granny over any way he could. After their rebellious marriage, Dad thought he could smooth ruffled feathers by converting to Catholicism. He dutifully went to see the local parish priest to begin the process, which turned out to be very brief. After just a couple of sessions of indoctrination, Dad told the priest to go where no priest ever should, and stomped out of his office. My mother wound up becoming a Protestant.

As a result of her strict upbringing, Mother harbored feelings of resentment against our grandmother. Sometimes she painted Granny, who seemed to us like such a sweet little old lady, as a stern taskmaster. She told us of having to sit and embroider tablecloths and crochet doilies in the evenings instead of going out with friends. She complained of waiting on fussy customers and stocking shelves in the store instead of meeting boys and going dancing. And instead of sitting in a beauty salon to get her own hair done, she spent her Saturdays shampooing other women's hair and sweeping up in her sister's shop. She saw her little brother Joe as the favored child, the spoiled baby of the family, and she was unhappy about having to watch over him and wait on him when he was sick. Jealous of her two older sisters who got the opportunity to go to college while she was stuck in the role of Cinderella at home, she felt overlooked and over worked. Since for her there was no fairy godmother to intervene, when someone who resembled Prince Charming came along, Mother seized the chance and ran off with him.

After her hasty marriage, she gave all her energy to her new family. Once she had made her decision, she stuck with it and wound up sacrificing everything for us for the rest of her life. Growing up, she had learned the lessons of hard work, honesty, and perseverance. Unfortunately, she had not learned independence, self confidence, or assertiveness. Later, when the time came for her to stand up for Bev, she didn't have the tenacity to question or challenge. Instead, she was unfailingly polite and compliant and honest and trusting. She never learned that sometimes it doesn't pay to be nice. It would have been helpful if Dad could have provided the assurance that Mother lacked, but in the self esteem department, he was no better off than she was.

Our father, John, was born in Reading, Pennsylvania in 1921 to parents of German descent, their first and only child together. His young mother Maude died when he was only two years old, leaving his father to cope on his own with an active toddler. His father had a younger sister, Ruth, who was still living with their parents at the time of Maude's death. Dad was placed in that household to be looked after by both his grandparents and aunt, who took care of him while his father worked to feed the family and to rebuild his life after losing his wife. This supposedly temporary arrangement soon became permanent, and Ruth gradually took over the role of parent, raising Dad as if he were her own child. As time went on, his father became less and less involved with him, and their relationship grew ever more distant.

Eventually our grandfather became involved with another woman and remarried. He and his new wife set up their own household, one that did not include Dad, and raised a son there. Even though the two boys were technically step brothers, they barely got to know each other. They grew up like strangers, in separate homes. We heard occasional references to this mysterious uncle in conversation, but we never met him, and Dad rarely spoke of him. Not surprisingly, Dad carried a bitter seed in his heart for his father's rejection and apparent preference for his second family. His father's lack of affection just reinforced the feelings of abandonment that had begun with his mother's death, and those feelings plagued him for the rest of his life.

When we were children, Dad and his father had apparently made peace enough so that we could visit on occasion, but our grandfather seemed like a stranger to us and his wife had no affection at all for Dad or his brood. She ignored us as if we didn't exist. When we did visit their home, we children sat stiffly on the sofa in their stuffy living room, afraid to move or speak unless spoken to. Even Dad, the perpetual charmer, was ill at ease. They had a little black and white Boston terrier that we loathed. She was the darling of the household, allowed to sniff us and jump on us and growl at us at her pleasure. I am a dog lover, but to this day Boston terriers make me wrinkle my nose. They doted on her, though, and she returned the favor. It seems appropriate that when our grandfather died suddenly from a massive heart attack after taking her for a walk, she was by his side.

In reality it was Aunt Ruth who raised Dad and devoted herself to his care and well being. Although she eventually did get married, she never had children of her own. She was a tall, statuesque woman, very attractive and glamorous. With her smart clothes and glittery jewelry and fur coats, she looked like a movie star. Her choice of husband however, was an odd one. She married a short, thin, Milquetoast fellow who always smelled of whiskey and spoke so softly you could barely hear him. They lived in a small apartment decorated with white rugs, blonde furniture, and mid century knick knacks including lidded crystal dishes filled with stale candy. Ruth adored our father and affectionately called him Mugsy. To her, he was a son, and we were her grandchildren. It was Aunt Ruth who always made sure we had Christmas gifts and Easter baskets and birthday presents, and who provided financial help to our father when he was down and out. Though she did her best to make up for his loss, he never got over his abandonment by his real mother and the later rejection by his father.

Dad never matured emotionally, and he held on to his childhood trauma for the rest of his life. His quest for love in all the wrong places never failed to ruin all his close relationships. When he married our mother, like her, he felt that he was breaking out to start a new life. He had high hopes for the house with the white picket fence, where he hoped to find the security he craved in a family of his own making. Unfortunately, his emotional scars held him back, and he was never able to leave the past behind no matter how bright the future might look. Dad spent his life mourning the loss of his mother, whom he revered as an angelic figure who had loved him dearly. In his mind she was perfect, and he set her on a pedestal that no other woman could ever reach.

When Beverley was born, home was a small post war tract house in Pennside, near Reading, Pennsylvania. Although this was her first home, she wouldn't really remember it, because when she was about four years old, the family left that house and moved in with our Aunt Florence. That is the first home Bev can really recall. She remembers living in her red brick Victorian row house on Tenth Street in the city of Reading and still talks about our Aunt Florence with great affection.

Although we always called her "Aunt Florence", she wasn't our aunt at all, but actually our father's cousin. During our short stay in her home we all developed a close relationship with her that continued until her death. Despite the fact that she was feisty, opinionated, and stubborn, we all grew to love her dearly. She was the peculiar old "aunt" who became an important part of our childhood experience, a quintessential old maid, living alone in her parents' house, surrounded by Victorian antiques and memories. The beautiful furnishings in the house spoke of a prosperous time, yet as the years went on after her father's death, she wound up living in poverty. Since she never had a job, she lived primarily on her inheritance from her father, insurance, and a few meager social security checks. By the time we came to stay with her, the house had already fallen into disrepair and neglect, while she was in failing health and living like a hermit. Somehow our father managed to talk her into taking us in. The promise of rent money was probably the only reason she even considered it.

I was born shortly after our family moved in with her. Flossie made it clear that having a baby in the house was not going to agree with her in the least. However, Mother claimed that once I was born, my aunt couldn't resist me and wound up fussing over me and welcoming me after all. Once we had all descended upon our aunt, the house must certainly have been crowded, with just three bedrooms for six people, one of them an infant. On top of that, the house definitely was not child friendly. It was dark and gloomy, with steep stairs for us to fall down and a hot coal stove in the kitchen to burn ourselves on. Every room was crammed with the formal Victorian furniture and delicate knick knacks she had inherited from her parents, nothing moved or rearranged since her father passed away. The dimly lit front parlor was rarely used, though we children were sometimes allowed to go in to plunk on the out of tune upright piano during our Sunday visits in later years. The room smelled of musty rugs and mothballs and furniture polish. It looked like a museum.

The house was arranged in typical fashion for a turn of the century row home. Heavy double front doors with leaded glass windows opened into a vestibule, followed by a long hallway that led past the parlor with its French doors on the right, straight back into the dining room where an impressive stained glass lamp trimmed with beads hung over a huge round oak table. There was a hallway on the second floor directly above the one on the first floor. At the top of the main hall staircase was a small back bedroom which could also be entered by the narrow winding kitchen stairs. Attached to this bedroom was a dilapidated sun porch that looked out onto the overgrown garden below. Down the hallway were two more bedrooms, one the master bedroom, Flossie's inner sanctum, with a massive carved wooden bed and other elaborate Victorian pieces. The other bedroom was a bit smaller and plainer, with a creaky iron double bed and sparse furnishings. At the end of the hall was a black and white tiled bathroom, beautiful but barely functional, with rust stained porcelain and leaky plumbing.

The kitchen in the rear of the house was positively Dickensian, with a slate sink, an old fashioned ice box, and a big coal stove for both cooking and providing heat. Because the central heating was no longer in working order, the kitchen was the only warm room in the house. There also was no hot water. I remember our mother telling us how she had to heat kettles of water on the coal stove in order for anyone to have a warm bath upstairs. One evening while Mother was hauling a pot of steaming water up the narrow back stairs, Bev ran up behind her and she accidentally dumped the hot water on her. Poor Bev was scalded and undoubtedly badly frightened. Since it was one of the few stories Mother told about that time, it must have been a traumatic event. That incident came to symbolize the struggle that living there presented for her, and she carried the bitter memory with her always.

A door led from the kitchen into a typical row home backyard, long and narrow, with a cement walk that led to a paved alley lined with the tiny garages that sat at the end of each property. Directly behind the house was a grape arbor that was heavy and fragrant with dark blue concord grapes in the summertime. A long neglected kitchen garden, overgrown with weeds and a few pathetic rose bushes, lined the wire fence that separated her yard from the neighbors' patch. The earliest existing photograph of myself was taken in that yard, apparently soon after I arrived on the scene. My mother is holding me, beaming with pride as she pulls a blanket away from my face for the camera. We both look very happy. Another photo, taken a bit later, shows me bundled against the cold in a snowsuit as I sat on a little wooden sled. We stayed on through the winter months, while Greg finished his kindergarten year at the neighborhood school, before we left for greener pastures elsewhere.

Even after we had moved out of Aunt Florence's house, we remained close to her and visited often. In later years I remembered that house fondly, with its smell of linoleum in the dim kitchen, the soothing ticking of the grandfather clock, the sound of water constantly dripping into the pan under the icebox. Sometimes Aunt Florence baby-sat for Jonnie and me when our parents went out for the evening. When she felt up to it, she would walk us up the alley behind her house, out onto Tenth Street to a corner store for ice cream. We skipped back home as Aunt Florence huffed and puffed behind us, then sat in the kitchen eating our treat and listening to the hypnotic ticking of the clock as the setting sun streamed in through the filmy kitchen window. We all sat at the table and played "Uncle Wiggly" until dark, when Jonnie and I would curl up and fall asleep on the soft worn leather couch in the corner by the stove to wait for our parents to scoop us up and take us home.

These things that make up nostalgic memories for us must have made our mother's life there miserable. She is the one who had to do the washing with no hot water and the cooking on an ancient coal stove and the hauling of kettles of water in that cold and dreary place. It was no picnic for her in that old house, with no conveniences and three children and a husband and cranky aunt to care for. She had no fond memories. But Aunt Florence truly loved us all in her cantankerous way, and she especially cherished forlorn little Beverley all her life long.

When our parents first got married, they had high hopes for their life together, though, in reality, neither of them was prepared for marriage and children and the financial burden of providing for a family. Nonetheless, they plunged headfirst into married life. As the years went by, photographs from the family album show Greg and Bev as toddlers enjoying what to outward appearances was a normal childhood. Dad snapped pictures as they ran through the rose gardens in a nearby park and smiled for the camera in their Sunday best clothes. In 1947 I joined the group and posed with them in front of the family car as we spent an afternoon in the country or took our Aunt Florence to the cemetery to plant flowers. We were all smiling, enjoying the simple pleasures of an ordinary post war life in small town America. These photographs freeze happy moments in time, but they were only moments. The reality is not reflected there. The reality is that Bev was not the happy, carefree child she appears to be. The truth is that Bev was an intellectually disabled little girl who struggled to keep up with her siblings, even though our mother tried to will her to fit into a normal life. By the time I was born, Mother had already spent over a year trying to find out what was causing Bev's problems. She knew something was very wrong and, most likely at the suggestion of our trusted family doctor, went out to seek medical help. Her quest for answers began when she first took Bev to the Pediatric Department of the Reading Hospital. This is how the journey begins.

Mother first brought Bev to the Reading Hospital Pediatric Department to be treated for anemia in April of 1946, a couple of months shy of her third birthday. As they rode the bus together clear across town and over the river to the hospital in West Reading, they had no idea what a long and perilous journey lay ahead. Though Bev's developmental problems were obvious to our parents by then, they may have been hoping for her to "grow out of it" and somehow catch up. Whatever the case, this hospital visit was the first formal step to find out what was really going on. It also produced the first official chronicle of Bev's physical and mental retardation. The doctors' report says that she was small for her age, didn't eat well, and had always been pale. She also seemed to have poor vision and held objects close to her face. That part of the diagnosis was fairly straightforward. The pediatrician ordered blood work and referred Bev to the eye clinic and neurological department. Both of those departments, however, had difficulty evaluating her because of her young age and lack of cooperation. The blood work showed some anemia, which was then treated with iron supplements and thyroid medication, both of which seemed to help her gain weight. The real difficulty came when Mother revealed that Bev was "backward", barely talking at age two years and ten months. This was far more puzzling.

The doctors at the hospital were looking for a physical reason for her problems, but were unable to find any. After a full physical examination, an eye exam, and extensive blood work, the doctors found nothing wrong other than mild anemia and muscle atonicity, which is a lack of muscle tone. The fact that Bev didn't walk until she was almost two years old would certainly account for underdeveloped muscles. Once she was walking, that actually began to correct itself. Family photos of Bev as a young child show her to be thin, but with no obvious muscle atrophy, and some snapshots even show her running. One doctor from the neuro-psychiatry clinic concluded that:

> I do not feel that there is any organic Central Nervous system disease other than possible oligophrenia (lack of mental development). The child is too uncooperative to thoroughly investigate this phase psychologically. Diagnosis held in abeyance pending further observation.

Though Bev continued to be seen at regular intervals, I didn't find any evidence showing that Bev was examined further by any psychologist or psychiatrist at the hospital. No one ever came up with any sort of psychiatric diagnosis, and no one even seemed to consider her uncooperative behavior to actually be part of a diagnosis. Someone eventually referred her to a place called the Guidance Institute of Reading, but I have no idea what happened there. All mental examinations that I read about were conducted by a psychologist connected with the Reading School District. Mother was obviously trying her best to get Bev help, but, unfortunately in those days, the extent and quality of help was limited. The Reading Hospital was a good hospital with an accredited nursing school. However, had our parents been able to see physicians at one of the more prestigious hospitals in nearby Philadelphia, would they have gotten better answers? They might have, but sixty years ago doctors simply didn't have many answers for mental disabilities. Quite frankly, none of the tests or examinations indicated any extreme physical problems or any obvious reason for her retarded development. Despite their best efforts, the help the doctors at the Reading Hospital were able to give Bev was minimal. After three years of treatment, her problems finally came to a head when she tried to attend school in the fall of 1949.

Our family left Aunt Florence's house in the summer of 1948 when Bev was five years old and moved to Mohnton, a small borough on the outskirts of Reading. Since Bev has only a few memories of living with Aunt Florence, she considers the house in Mohnton as her real childhood home, the "home" in her dreams. This is the place where she spent four years of her life, from age five to age nine. This would be the place where most of her childhood memories were formed and where most of her early education took place. This was the last place on earth where she lived a normal life.

The atmosphere when we lived there was blue collar, most of the homes modest, the countryside just a stone's throw beyond its orderly streets. On the edge of town a trolley car line ran to the center of the city of Reading. There was an elementary school not far from our house and a junior/senior high school a bit further away, but still within walking distance. There were a few small businesses, a supermarket, and a pretzel factory with a little stream running underneath it. Our house was set precariously on a steep hillside right on the main street of the town. It was an odd, rundown house that my father tried to fix up with very little money and not much home improvement skill. His most bizarre project was nailing bark covered logs onto the walls of the living room to make it look like a log cabin. Though he meant it as a creative statement, it was more a reminder that we lived like poor log cabin folk struggling to make ends meet.

The backyard was where we children spent much of our time. Long and narrow, it consisted of more bare dirt than grass, but it was a good place to ride our tricycles and play games. On the hill above the yard itself was a grove of trees where we also could play. Mother sometimes sat outside with us at a tree shaded table in the summertime, with a pitcher of lemonade and maybe a treat of homemade candy or cookies. Very few photos taken at that house remain, but there are some that feature Bev at ages six, seven, and eight. One shows my mother and grandmother posing by the picket fence with Greg, Bev, me and even our Springer Spaniel, Rex. Another photo evoked a gasp from both my husband and myself when we saw that Bev was holding a baseball bat, perhaps not the best idea, as she played with me in the yard. One of my favorites is of Greg pushing me, bundled in a snowsuit, on a sled while Bev stands by watching in her matching woolen pants and coat and sporting a flowered babushka.

So that my mother had time to get her chores done, Greg and I were often assigned to keep Bev occupied. As I think back, I can see myself sitting upstairs in that house on a bare wooden floor playing games with Beverley. I don't remember much about what we played together, but I do know that my main concern was letting her win at the games and keeping her calm so that she didn't have a tantrum. She would hit and pinch me when she got angry, so a lot of our play was self defense on my part. I can say that I did not entirely enjoy playing with her. To make matters worse, from my point of view, was the fact that I also had a baby sister to entertain. Once Jonnie started walking, my mother really had her hands full trying to manage both an active baby and Bev, whose mental age was that of a toddler. She needed all the help she could get, and Greg and I often had to pitch in to do our part.

Despite the fact that our house was shabby and food was sometimes scarce, Bev was happy being at home and living with her family around her. We were poor, no doubt about it, but in the late forties and early fifties that wasn't unusual. In the wake of the war, with economic prosperity yet to come, everyone was struggling financially. We were just another family trying to make it through. Though the rest of us may look back on these years as hard scrabble times, to Bev these were the happy days that she would always remember and treasure. Mohnton was the house she left when she went away to stay at the facility at Pennhurst. This was the home she wanted to return to.

From the moment she set foot in Pennhurst she talked constantly about coming home, but while she was away the family home had changed many times. Throughout the years, although we took her to wherever we were living at the time, to Bev "home" was the house in Mohnton, and no other place was quite the same. Even though we believed we were taking her home for her visits, once we left Mohnton, I don't think Bev ever really went home again. Even today when she is sitting with us and eating a holiday meal or opening Christmas gifts or blowing out the candles on a birthday cake, she still talks about going home. I believe she is still waiting to return there. All the other homes just aren't real. To her, "home" is the memory of playing happily in the backyard of the rickety old house in Mohnton. Nothing else will ever be right.

While we were living there, Bev attempted to go to public school three years in a row, starting at the age of six. Her first try at kindergarten was in September of 1949. In those days everyone walked to school, whether it was an urban neighborhood school or a small town school like ours. Our elementary school building was just a few blocks from our house, within easy walking distance. It was a two story stone structure that had a small asphalt play area on one side with a jungle gym, see saw and swings. I can imagine Mother on the first day of school, dressing Bev up in her Sunday best, combing her hair, buckling her shoes, then holding her hand tightly as she walked her up the street, praying under her breath that Bev would be in a cooperative mood. Unfortunately, those prayers were not answered. I'm sure that Bev wasn't the only little girl who cried and clung to her mother's skirt that first day. But unlike the other children, who eventually settled in to the school routine, Bev never stopped crying. She was not the least bit happy in school and lashed out at the teacher, as well as the other children. She refused to follow directions, biting and screaming and banging her head against the wall in frustration. Though the teacher tried to give Bev time to quiet down, she soon realized that there was more going on than she could handle. Because of her uncontrollable behavior, Bev continued attending class for only a few days before she was sent to see a school district psychologist for evaluation.

The psychologist who saw her seems to have been a very caring and sympathetic woman who was sincerely trying to help Mother get Bev into school. According to the therapist, her first meeting with Bev "yielded nothing in the way of test results." Apparently, Bev was so uncooperative that she couldn't even be tested successfully. She wanted nothing to do with strangers who gave her orders and asked her endless questions. Mother had no choice but to keep her at home and work with her on her own until a few months later, in January of 1950, when the psychologist tried testing her again and had better success. After that meeting, she must have recommended that Mother give Bev some time to mature before she tried school again. Bev was seven years old when September rolled around and she found herself in a kindergarten classroom for the second time. Just like before, she lasted only a few days and wound up in the psychologist's office for the third time in twelve months.

The examination this time around was more extensive and yielded a lot more information about Bev. The psychologist says in her report that Bev was better behaved, her speech had improved, and she was wearing eyeglasses. These developments made testing her much easier. After a battery of mental development tests, the psychologist recorded an I.Q. of 43. According to modern standards, an I.Q. of 70 is considered the benchmark for mental retardation, which is then broken down into categories of mild, moderate, severe, and profound. A score of 43 would have put Bev in the category of moderate to severe retardation. How accurate that test result was, however, is uncertain. Persuading Bev to test well was a problem that would crop up throughout her life. When Bev was cooperative she could perform fairly well on the tests, but most of the time she stubbornly refused to answer or do what she was asked to do. Once she retreated into her shell, it was nearly impossible to get her to respond.

Beyond the test results, the psychologist offers some personal observations in her report. Remarkably, she doesn't seem to have much of a professional vocabulary. Instead, she calls Bev's behavior "strange." She observed that Bev twisted and jerked and stared off into space at times. Not surprisingly, much later in life, Bev was diagnosed with Tourette Syndrome. Although the term is not used, the psychologist goes on to describe signs of obsessive/compulsive behavior, also diagnosed by doctors much later. She also says that Bev often engaged in marked echolalia, echoing back what was said to her. This is definitely not unusual in someone with OCD.

Finally, the psychologist concludes that "I have observed little purposeful behaviour on the part of this child other than her resistance."

The Journey Begins

This just doesn't sound like someone who has a real understanding of what she was observing. Did she really think that Bev was consciously trying to give her a hard time? Bev was frightened, stressed by having a stranger press her for answers to questions she found meaningless. A mentally challenged child like Bev would have trouble understanding most of what was being asked, let alone coming up with an acceptable answer.

I have no way of knowing what was decided between the psychologist and Mother after this evaluation session. I only know that Mother was desperate for Bev to be able to attend public school. If she couldn't, she wouldn't be able to stay at home. Mother had three other children to care for, including a new baby. She had to work to help put food on the table and pay the mortgage. She didn't have the time, energy, or resources to take care of Bev full time. Bev would have to go to a special school, and for a family like ours, a state institution was the only possible solution. If special education classes had been available in public schools in those days, Bev would never have had to go to Pennhurst State School.

In one last attempt to find some hope in Bev's diagnosis, the school psychologist later consulted with a more experienced professional, a female psychiatrist, in July of 1951. By then Bev was eight years old and still had not attended public school for more than a few days. Not surprisingly, Bev tested well below her capabilities. Here was yet another stranger badgering her with questions, expecting her to sit still and count and write and answer, answer, answer. Again, the stressful situation got the best of Bev, and she performed poorly. Even though Mother told the doctor that Bev actually was able to do many of the things she failed to do during the testing, the doctor came to the conclusion that Bev was never going to be able to learn much of anything. She obviously held out no hope for Bev in a public school classroom. She wrote in her report that "this child has considerable difficulty adjusting to any new situation. She is completely lost in a competitive atmosphere."

It is heartbreaking to read her statement. What worse place could there be for a child like Bev, who could not adapt to change and who could not function in a group situation, than an institution like Pennhurst State School? But this is exactly what this psychiatrist, hospital doctors, and public school officials obviously recommended, because less than a month later, on August 18, 1951, our mother wrote a letter to Pennhurst requesting an application for admission. Yet, even as she filled out the forms, Mother still hoped for a miracle, because in September 1951 she enrolled Bev in first grade at the local public school. She lasted just nine days.

~2~

The Place at the End of the World

Construction began on the *Eastern Pennsylvania State Institution for the Fee-ble-Minded and Epileptic in 1903* on approximately 600 acres of rolling farmland along the Schuylkill River, near the community of Spring City, PA, which is about 40 miles north of Philadelphia. Later known as Pennhurst State School, then Pennhurst State School and Hospital, and finally the Pennhurst Center, this institution was home to thousands of intellectually disabled men, women, and children for nearly eighty years. The first group of buildings, called the "lower campus", was completed in 1908, and on November 23 of that year patient "number one" was admitted. Those original buildings, constructed of neat rows of red brick with sculpted granite trim, were beautifully designed. The center-piece was the grand administration building, topped with a stately copper cupola. The two story Jacobean Revival buildings were connected by a network of concrete walkways, while hidden far beneath them lay a dark maze of underground tunnels. The sprawling campus stood out impres-sively among the surrounding green fields of the Pennsylvania country-side. Little did the architects know what suffering these imposing struc-tures would someday hold.

The first buildings put in place on the lower campus were identified only by letter designations. Building "G", for instance, was the kitchen and store room. "H", "I", and "K" were cottages for girls while "Q", "T", "U" and "V" were cottages for boys ,"F" was the Girl's Dining

Room, "N" was the Boys' Dining Room, "P" was the Teachers Home, "R" was a School, "W" was the Laundry, and 'X' was the Power House. When the buildings on the upper campus were completed in 1930, they were given the names Pershing, Buchanan, Audubon, and Keystone. By 1979, the older buildings that still had only the letter designations followed suit and took on names corresponding to the letters already assigned, such as "Quaker" for the "Q" building.

ADMINISTRATION BUILDING

By the 1950's the grounds had expanded to cover over 1200 acres. Even though much of the land was cultivated farmland, there were also over 80 buildings, and Pennhurst had turned into a huge institutional complex. Seventeen of these structures were residence halls that became filled as fast as they could be built. Construction was never able to keep up with the demand, and there was always a waiting list. Overcrowding was a serious problem from the very day the doors opened. Unfortunately for Bev, when she was admitted to Pennhurst in 1952, the overcrowding was at its worst with the population approaching its highest levels ever.

The history of Pennhurst is a sad and complicated one. In order to understand what happened there, it's important to know what the attitudes of society were when Pennhurst was first established. In the early twentieth century, developmentally disabled people were considered deviants who needed to be kept away from the rest of society and prevented from procreating. They were blamed for many problems such as public drunkenness, crime, and poverty. Institutions like Pennhurst were built to protect society from the mentally deficient by locking them away. Such institutions were intended to be used to warehouse these people with the idea that they were little better than animals and didn't need much in the way of comfort. All they needed was a bed, some food, and minimal medical care. It was believed that their mental impairment made them subhuman creatures oblivious to the conditions in which they were made to live. Only limited attempts were made to educate them or provide them with any opportunities to improve their lives. If possible, they were taught to do some menial tasks such as farm labor, domestic chores, or handicrafts. Otherwise they were considered hopeless and were sentenced to a meaningless existence.

In the early twentieth century when Pennhurst opened, modern psychology was still in its infancy. It was at this time that the first attempts were being made to study mental retardation, then referred to as feeblemindedness. Some of the pioneers in this field were Alfred Binet, Theodore Simon, William Stern, and Henry Goddard. The work of these four men broke new ground as they created a process for the measurement of intellectual ability. Alfred Binet, a French psychologist, worked with his partner Theodore Simon to develop the first intelligence test in 1905 to help identify children who were in need of special education. A few years later, William Stern, a German psychologist, developed the Intelligence Quotient, or IQ, for measuring intelligence. His scale was then applied to the results of the Binet-Simon tests. Henry Goddard, an American psychologist and a pioneer in the field of clinical psychology, translated the Binet test into English in 1908 and distributed it for use in the United States. He devoted much of his career to studying feeblemindedness and was especially interested in testing methods. Goddard was largely responsible for developing the classifications for the mentally retarded that would be used for decades. Morons were individuals with an IQ between 51 and 70 and a mental age of 7 to 12, imbeciles had an IQ between 26 and 50 and a mental age of 3 to 7, and idiots had an IQ between 0 and 25 and a mental age below 3. Bev, with an IQ around 45, would have been considered an imbecile. The terms moron, imbecile, and idiot are now considered outdated and politically incorrect, but they were routinely used in the mental health field until the 1970's when new terminology was developed. People with developmental disabilities are now referred to in the field as mildly, moderately, severely, or profoundly retarded. In non medical settings, the term intellectual disability has now replaced the term mental retardation.

The work of men like Binet, Simon, Stern, and Goddard paved the way for the treatment and education of the mentally retarded, but progress was painfully slow, and many mistakes occurred along the way. Their research was done in the early days of the fledgling field of psychology; it would take many years for others to build on their insights into mental retardation and to find humane and effective ways of dealing with it. In the meantime, places like Pennhurst were considered state-of-the-art facilities ready to handle the problem of the feebleminded members of society. Unfortunately, Henry Goddard, who did so much good work in the field, said early in his career that every feebleminded person is a potential criminal. Though he later revised that position, it nevertheless remained the prevailing belief for many years. That meant that the first step was to separate such people from normal, law abiding citizens. The people in public institutions for the mentally disabled were called "inmates", as if they were criminals in a prison. Though there were no gun towers or barbed wire fences, these places might as well have been penitentiaries - prisons for people whose only crime was being mentally retarded. For this crime, many were doomed to a life sentence of incarceration.

Because of this attitude of protecting society first and foremost, all sorts of people were sent to Pennhurst including violent, homicidal, or suicidal individuals and even convicted criminals. From the very beginning the first superintendent, H. M. Carey, complained about the inappropriate use of Pennhurst to house these types of people. In the first place, there was some dispute about caring for the epileptic and feeble minded in the same facility. Carey's opinion was that "They are not the same; they are as different from the other, as day is from night. They are mentally, physically and morally incompatible, and require entirely different treatment."

But beyond this, the term "feeble minded " was being misinterpreted to mean anyone that society considered deviant and wanted to lock away. No distinction was made between mental retardation and mental illness or socially aberrant behavior, let alone epilepsy and feeblemindedness. Socially unacceptable people were being sent in such great numbers that Pennhurst became overcrowded within a few months of its opening. As soon as residential buildings were completed, they were filled beyond their recommended capacity. In its first year of operation in 1908 the patient population grew rapidly to about 150, and in less than fifty years had reached over 3500.

With its ever growing number of residents, as well as hospital staff and maintenance workers, Pennhurst became like a small town with dozens of buildings and hundreds of acres of land. In more ways than one, Pennhurst State School became a world unto itself. From its early days, the institution strove to be self sufficient. In addition to the large administration building and residence halls, there were recreation areas, several kitchens and dining rooms, a library, a hospital, and even a cemetery. Most of the land was farmed to grow fruits and vegetables, which were then canned on the premises. Chickens, pigs, and dairy cows were raised to provide eggs, meat, and milk. There was a power plant, machine shop, sewage disposal plant, garage, ice plant and laundry. Carpentry and tailor shops supplied almost all of the furniture and clothing, even mattresses. Much of the labor was done by unpaid resident workers supervised by paid staff, which helped keep costs down and provided occupational therapy at the same time. Pennhurst prided itself on providing everything its patients needed. Almost everything.

As year after year more people with special needs were admitted, feeding and clothing them were the least of the problems that presented themselves. Providing adequate housing was the biggest challenge, not only because of growing numbers, but also because of the wide range of disabilities represented among them. Many of the inmates had severe physical disabilities which confined them to beds or cribs. Less severe cases could move around in wheelchairs but still needed help with basic self care. Mental handicaps ranged from mildly retarded to profoundly retarded and even included many forms of depression and insanity. Thrown in with the intellectually disabled were juvenile delinquents and deranged criminals. Somehow this institution was expected to provide services for men, women, and children with an impossibly wide range of both physical and psychological needs. Basic care was enough of a challenge. Providing any sort of effective treatment or education was a daunting task.

With housing a challenge from the very beginning, construction continued into the 1920's in an effort to keep up with demand. Even so, residence halls remained filled to overflowing. Beds were closely crammed into wards, and even bunk beds were used to provide enough places to sleep. Though new admissions continued on a regular basis, only one new building was erected during the Depression years, and none during World War II. After the War, two buildings already planned were completed, but no new buildings were added between 1950 and 1970. In 1926 the patient population was around 1200 and by 1955 had risen to 3500. While the resident population had almost tripled in those intervening thirty years, new construction had slowed until it eventually ground to a halt. It doesn't take much imagination to understand how conditions ultimately became overcrowded to the point of being inhumane.

On top of the problems related to overcrowding was the lack of sufficient funds to operate the facility. It was up to the state legislature to allocate the money to properly care for the inmates, and their per capita allotment was far below what was needed. Every superintendent from the very beginning pled the case for more money. There was not enough money for new construction, for equipment, for doctors and nurses, for teachers and classrooms, for support staff. In 1955, for example, with a resident population of 3500, there were just FOUR psychologists in their "up-to-date" Psychology Department. These problems, evident from the very inception of Pennhurst, existed until the 1970's when reform measures finally began to change the way the institution operated. By then Pennhurst had become a nightmare.

Unfortunately, in the first half of the twentieth century, parents of intellectually disabled children had few choices, and despite their misgivings, continued to place their children in the care of large institutions like Pennhurst. Information booklets distributed to families in the 1940's and 1950's depicted Pennhurst as an almost idyllic existence for the children who were sent to live there. Looking at these booklets myself, I can understand how our parents could have read this literature and come away believing that Pennhurst was absolutely the right place to send Bev to be protected, cared for, educated, and prepared to take a limited place in society some day. Between looking at the pamphlets and talking to the social workers and doctors, I'm sure they felt that, despite their misgivings about sending Bev away, they were doing what was ultimately in her best interests. What was depicted in the pamphlets was someone's idea of what an institution for developmentally disabled children should be like. In reality, it was a grand idea that bore little resemblance to the truth, and the parents who believed it were cruelly deceived.

The pamphlets make fascinating reading in light of what we know now to be the truth. They are sadly misguided pieces of propaganda showcasing the wonderful world of Pennhurst. They are full of photographs peopled by dozens of staff, from doctors and nurses to agriculture and maintenance workers. Perfectly staged photographs show young residents engaging in activities ranging from volleyball to musical groups to picnics. The children are clean and well dressed, but one thing is immediately evident. Few of them are smiling. The ones who are have pasted on smiles that don't reflect any true feeling. They are children much like Bev. Even today, when we are taking a photo and ask Bev to smile, she instantly smiles broadly and stays that way until we tell her she can stop posing. The smile means nothing. She's just following directions. To the casual observer the photos show happy children. We now know better.

That's not to say that every resident of Pennhurst was unhappy. For some of them life at Pennhurst was better than their life at home, for some it was the only home they could remember, for some the staff provided more love than they had ever before received, for some the routine of institutional life provided the security and structure they craved. For some it actually worked. But for the overwhelming majority it did not, even though the booklets gave the impression it did.

By the 1940's Pennhurst's name had long since been changed from the Eastern Pennsylvania Institution for the Epileptic and Feebleminded to Pennhurst State School, yet the information pamphlets always referred to the residents as "patients", never as students. Page seven of the 1940's pamphlet explains it this way: "Pennhurst State School is at the same time a hospital and a school, having the dual purpose of providing adequate custody for all patients and of providing all necessary facilities for diagnosis, treatment, education, and training." This reflects the prevailing attitude that intellectually disabled people are somehow sick because of a lack of "normally functioning brain cells" and are considered defective and deficient.

Nevertheless, this booklet from the 1940's is upbeat and chatty, emphasizing the felicitous life led by the young patients. After a brief overview of the institution, it tells parents how to apply and states the rules and regulations for visiting and sending mail or gifts. It was meant to provide easy-to-read information that would show Pennhurst in a positive light. The opening letter to the parents in this pamphlet is sympathetic and reassuring, with a final paragraph that tries to put parents' minds at ease about their decision. After reading it, how could any parents suspect that sending their child to Pennhurst wasn't their wisest alternative?

> Thus, if you have left your child at the Pennhurst State School in our care, or are planning to do so, let me urge you to disabuse your mind of needless worry or feeling of parental guilt. The Commonwealth of Pennsylvania has provided very remarkable facilities of all kinds for the welfare, treatment, and education of your unfortunate boy or girl. If the outlook for the child is hopeless for training, you will be given expert advice to this effect and we shall do all that is medically possible to make him happy and comfortable. And, if the outlook is hopeful, let me say that when you leave your child in our hospital, rather than feel you have sealed his doom, be assured you have probably opened a gate to many opportunities for him.

This sounds like a wonderful promise, but for Bev it was an empty one. There was no gate to opportunities for her. For her, and certainly for hundreds of other children like her, all gates and doors and windows literally remained locked as long as Pennhurst was her home. Her outlook should have been hopeful, but it was not. As I got older and mulled it over, I wondered how our parents could have sent Bev to

Pennhurst. I couldn't imagine that anyone would want to send a child to such a place. However, after looking at the pamphlets that they surely must have read as part of their indoctrination, I can see how they were led to believe that Pennhurst was their best hope. If they could have seen what the future held for her, they never would have sent her there. How could they know?

The revised version of the pamphlet produced in 1954 is more formal and attempts to show Pennhurst's professional proficiency. It emphasizes statistics and is filled with photographs of no nonsense staff running a well oiled hospital machine. It characterizes Pennhurst as a state of the art facility providing excellent care for its clients. It doesn't explain how just four psychologists can adequately treat 3500 mentally handicapped patients or how only 360 nurses and attendants can cater to their every need. It doesn't explain how those 3500 residents can live comfortably in a facility meant to hold around 2000. It fails to mention the critical overcrowding, lack of adequate staff, and an insufficient budget that parents had a right to know about. Instead, it paints a picture of a safe and nurturing environment for intellectually disabled children and adults. The introduction written by the Superintendent, William Phillips, states:

> Not infrequently, the grief of the parent is greater than the unhappiness of the mentally defective child. Every doctor on our staff understands and appreciates the degree of affection which a parent naturally develops for the unfortunate child, and it is our wish to cooperate with parents in the same personal manner as would your private family physician. Furthermore, our extensive experience has taught us to share with you the personal sensitivity you most likely have been caused to feel, due to misunderstanding of the nature and causes of mental deficiency and the wagging tongues of misunderstanding neighbors or both.

The references to the child as "unfortunate" and "defective" reflect the overall attitude of grief and pity that the parents were expected to feel. The mention of the "wagging tongues" of neighbors reflects the attitude not only of society at large but even the extended family of the "defective" child. Parents of such children were made to feel that fate had saddled them with a great burden and that institutions like Pennhurst were intended to lift that burden from them and let them live their lives without the stigma of a "defective" child within the family. Parents were led to believe that their children were better off at Pennhurst than out in a world that did not understand or want them.

No matter what the original intent was for these institutions, they did not serve their disabled residents well. Most of them, not only in Pennsylvania but throughout the entire country, became overcrowded human warehouses, eventually unable to adequately provide basic care let alone meaningful training and education. However, despite the appalling conditions and the difficulties they faced, the administration and staff at Pennhurst believed that they were providing an important service to people who had "mentally deficient" family members and they tried to do their best to care for every one of them. They remind me of the orchestra on the deck of the Titanic, bravely playing on as the ship inevitably sank beneath the waves. They did their jobs as best they could against overwhelming odds. Many truly cared for their patients. No one who didn't would continue to work in such conditions. This was the state of public mental health care in the United States in the mid twentieth century. This was Pennhurst State School and Hospital. This was the place that took possession of nine-year-old Beverley Lynne Miller on June 11, 1952 and held her there for 32 years.

~3~

Down the Rabbit Hole

By September 1951 Mother had finally reached the end of the line. There was no where else to go. Bev's plunge down the rabbit hole began as the ink dried on the signatures at the end of the "Application for the Reception and Detention of the Within Alleged Mental Defective." Ironically, this application for admission to Pennhurst was completed and filed on October 31, 1951 - a perfect date for a nightmare to begin.

Once it was clear that Bev was unable to function in a public school classroom, her fate was sealed. When she failed at her third attempt to attend public school, Mother ran out of options. Our brother Greg remembers the day that the principal of Mohnton's Elementary School came to the house to inform our parents that there was nothing his school could do to help their daughter. Our father's frustration burst forth in an angry tirade about the "one horse town" that had nothing to offer his child. Of course, it wasn't the principal's fault. In those days most school districts, especially in smaller districts, had no alternative programs for students with special needs, and legislation requiring them to do so was over two decades away. It would be 1975 before federal legislation was passed that guaranteed all children, regardless of ability, a free public education. In the 1950's, public schools were not required to accept students like Bev. Most parents were on their own to cope as best they could.

After looking at all the reports and examinations and other documents, I realize that Mom absolutely did all the right things to help Bev. She started working with both the medical and educational establishment in April 1946 and kept at it until June 1952 when Bev was finally admitted to Pennhurst. Apparently, with little help from her husband, she knocked herself out trying to get help for Bev. One glaring fact stood out to me as I read the reports of Bev's early treatment, the psychologists' tests, the home visits, and the final stages leading to Bev's admission to Pennhurst. It was always our mother who dealt with it all. There is no mention of our father's presence at appointments or meetings and no signatures of his on any of the paperwork involved in admitting Bev to Pennhurst. I have no way of knowing why. I do know for a fact that Dad was never fond of the medical establishment and would have been very reluctant to seek their help. My guess is that he did not approve of sending Bev to doctors, especially psychiatrists. The reports seem to support my theory since, in every one of them, there was virtually no mention of our father. The only time his name came up at all was on the social worker's report that stated his name and occupation. Most of the effort to help Bev came from our mother. After years of testing and examinations and questionnaires, in the end, it was she alone who signed the final application for Bev's admission to Pennhurst. Why wasn't our father more involved, and where was he while our mother traipsed from doctor to doctor and office to office on her own? Why wouldn't he have signed the admission papers for Pennhurst?

Whatever reasons Dad had for avoiding involvement with Bev's trek through the mental health system, the fact is that our parents were polar opposites when it came to dealing with the red tape involved in trying to diagnose and treat Bev. Dad had a stubborn disregard for authority and bucked the system in every way he could. School principals, teachers, and doctors all represented attempts to control his life. In his later years, he would join the Christian Scientists because of his extreme distrust of doctors and hospitals. He could not bring himself to believe that any of these people had his daughter's best interests at heart. Mother, on the other hand, was a staunch believer in going by the book. She trusted authority figures and tried to play by their rules. She would have believed that they were trying their best to help. As usual, the truth lay somewhere in between. The authority figures that our father rebelled against, the same ones our mother complied with, did try to help. But with limited resources at their disposal and no innovation to guide them, they all took the standard approach. In the end the system won - and failed them.

The most ironic part about Dad's lack of involvement with the quest to get help for Bev is the fact that Aunt Ruth, his surrogate mother, was one of the people behind the whole idea of sending Bev to Pennhurst. She loved Dad like a son, and there was nothing she wouldn't do for him. She felt that by encouraging him to send Bev to Pennhurst she was doing the best thing for him and his family. In 1951 she was working for the Social Services Department of Berks County. Familiar with the state residential institutions and the programs they offered, she also knew the procedures necessary for placing Bev at Pennhurst. It was very likely her advice and guidance that resulted in Bev's eventual admission there. Many people waited a long time for a chance to get into Pennhurst. Bev would have been considered one of the lucky ones.

The actual application for admission to Pennhurst appears to have been prepared by the staff at Pennhurst and then forwarded to the Reading Hospital, where a hospital psychiatrist filled out his portion of the form. In his part of the report, the psychiatrist states that Bev had been under treatment at the Neurological Clinic of Reading Hospital for a year and a half. He doesn't elaborate on what treatment she received at that clinic, except for the fact that she was given glutamic acid, which was sometimes used in the treatment of childhood behavioral disorders. The doctor seems to have relied heavily on the reports of the school district consultants in forming his opinion about Bev's condition, including her IQ. No matter how he came to his conclusions, he was obviously of the opinion that Bev belonged at Pennhurst and encouraged our parents to send her there. The application was ultimately signed by our mother, this doctor, and a Berks County Justice of the Peace.

Once the application had been filled out and submitted, the next step was a visit to our home in Mohnton by a social worker from Pennhurst. Her Social Service Report describes our family, our home, and the "patient". The report describes Bev's physical condition, activities, schooling and an entry called "peculiarities." This seems to be a quaint term for Bev's mental retardation, typical of the kind of language used in so many of the reports from that era. The social worker describes our house as being rundown and scantily furnished. It was obvious to her that our family's financial situation was dire. She was, however, impressed by the fact that our parents were both employed and were not alcoholics, something that she specifically points out. How she came to that conclusion, I have no idea, especially since Dad was no stranger to drink. However, she could tell that our mother was a good mother and, against tough odds, was doing her best to take care of her children. She states , "Although this family is struggling to combat financial problems, there is good supervision in the home; therefore, vacations are recommended."

In her conclusion, the social worker arrives at two main reasons for Bev to be admitted to Pennhurst. First was the fact that Bev had proved herself unable to attend public school. Second was the fact that Mother was having trouble dealing with her other children when Bev needed so much special attention. In the end she says, "I consider this defective child to be urgent for admission to Pennhurst."

She set the admission date for March 12, 1952.

In February of 1952, the hospital psychiatrist sent a lengthy letter to the Director of Social Service at Pennhurst State School. This rambling letter, which summarizes reports from the Reading Hospital pediatric department and from the psychologist representing the school district, seems to be a final presentation of the case for Bev's admission. Two facts from this letter strongly indicate that Mother was having a very difficult time making the final decision to send Bev to the institution and was not con-  vinced that sending Bev to Pennhurst was the best course of action.

First, although the admission date had already been set for March 12, 1952, Mother requested that the psychologist from the school district see Bev again in February. She obviously felt that Bev was showing improvement, and she was right. The report does clearly state that Bev performed much better at this time than she ever had before. Not only was her speech more coherent, but she also knew her colors and could count to 9. The psychologist found that she was more cooperative and did a better job on all her tests than she had previously. She writes, "Mother works with the child at home in an effort to teach her things which will help her general development. She has decided to visit Pennhurst and discuss problem."

At this meeting Mother intended to find out what Pennhurst could do for Bev that she could not. What would be the benefit to sending Bev there? What could justify separating a child from her home and family? In the end she must have been led to believe that Pennhurst would build on the education that she had begun at home and would also teach Bev new skills. Even though Mother had her doubts, it all sounded so promising.

Secondly, the psychiatrist from the Reading Hospital states in the final paragraph of his letter:

> It is my opinion that this child should very definitely be in your institution. Unfortunately the family has not been convinced and may waiver [sic] and refuse admission when an opening is available. I am trying to convince them to follow our recommendations.

Without a doubt, neither of our parents was ready to send Bev to Pennhurst. They had to be "convinced" to do so, and I have no doubt that many people worked hard to convince them. The psychiatrist from the Reading Hospital, the social service director from Pennhurst, the psychologist from the school district, as well as family members, especially Aunt Ruth, all had a hand in persuading them. They all had their reasons, but I don't understand why they were in such a hurry, why they didn't give Bev a little more time. When I look at the reports I get a picture of a child who seemed to be improving both intellectually and emotionally. But Bev always made testing difficult by being uncooperative. Even the school district psychologist, who tested her several times, said:

> Although this child is seriously retarded without any question of doubt, she may be considerably better than test results indicate at the present time. One of the major problems in the situation is her behavior.

Granted, Bev was achieving way below the level she should have been chronologically, but the important fact is that she was constantly improving. Our mother, with no training of any kind and little help from professionals, had done an admirable job of educating her daughter. To this day Bev still remembers much of it, and almost everything she can do or say academically came from Mother. I have never seen any evidence of her showing that she retained anything that Pennhurst tried to teach her in the classroom as a child. When asked her age, Bev will tell you she is six years old, and she performs mental tasks on the level of a kindergarten child. That's when Bev's intellectual life ended. Pennhurst not only didn't improve on what Bev came there with, but destroyed much of it. Our parents were right to have doubts about the rosy picture painted by Pennhurst.

Both of our parents rode an emotional roller coaster as they tried to make the final decision about how to help Bev. The documents show clearly that they agonized over their decision to send Bev to Pennhurst. Neither of them wanted to do it. Mother saw Bev's potential every day as she taught her at home and saw gradual improvements. Her behavior at home was so much better than at the hospital or in the psychologist's office. After the school district psychologist visited Bev at home she reported that "I have observed the child in her home when I have seen the mother and the child has been quiet and well-behaved." When the social worker from Pennhurst came to the house, she had the same impression. "At home, she [Bev] is rather quiet and shy and is not difficult for the mother to manage;"

Of course, Bev wasn't always easy to manage. Her panic attacks and tantrums often pushed her parents to the limits. As she grew bigger and stronger, her outbursts were more difficult to control. Dad admitted that he sometimes lost his temper with her and punished her for her naughty behavior. For the most part, though, Bev functioned well at home. Kudos to our mother. In difficult circumstances she was doing a stellar job.

By the time the Pennhurst social worker knocked on our door, our family's circumstances were grim. As often seems to be the case with people who are down and out, our family was plagued with trouble during these early years. It was as if a great, dark cloud hung over that house in Mohnton, and that what little we had was doomed to be taken away. It was an unlucky place for us, filled with tragedy and unhappiness. Our childhood years that should have been fun and carefree were gloomy and insecure. The overriding theme of our lives was poverty. Though relatives tried to help out, our parents were hard pressed to provide us with even the bare necessities. Mother often had to feed her children on "bread soup", small chunks of salted white bread floating in hot milk. I remember relishing those bowls of milk and bread as though they were a special treat. Little did I know that the reason we had such meals was that Mother was down to her last dollar and our cupboards were Old Mother Hubbard bare.

Even though their financial situation was precarious and they had a intellectually challenged daughter, Mother and Dad started having more babies. By the time Bev was school age my parents had four children; seven year old Greg, six year old Beverley, two year old Rory, and a new baby, Geoffrey. Tragically, little Geoffrey passed away suddenly in August 1949. Not long after his death, Mother became pregnant with Jonnie, her last baby, who was born in October of 1950. In the space of eight years Mother had given birth to five children, one of whom was developmentally disabled and one who died as an infant. She was physically and emotionally exhausted.

Somehow she found the strength to pursue every avenue she could to help Bev, working through the medical system for a period of six years, from the time she first set foot in the Pediatric Department of the Reading Hospital until Bev was finally admitted to Pennhurst. During those years of struggle and heartache, Mother went through three pregnancies and delivered three babies. As if that were not enough of a challenge, one of those babies, little Geoffrey, died at the age of two months. Just one month after his tragic death, Mother made her first attempt to enroll Bev in kindergarten and had to deal with that disappointing failure while still mourning the loss of her son.

Baby Geoffrey's death was always treated as something of a family mystery, a subject too painful for my mother to discuss. Sensitive children like myself don't like mysteries, especially when it comes to people dying. One day, at the age of two months, the baby suddenly developed a rash, swelling, and fever. The family doctor was called, but by the time he arrived, Geoffrey had already died in his mother's arms. The cause of death was listed as anaphylactic shock from an allergic reaction. Mother believed that he may have been stung by a bee or some other insect while she was out hanging wash with him lying in a stroller nearby. His tiny body was buried in a cemetery plot just a few feet from Dad's mother Maude. There is no headstone for him, just a thin carpet of grass. The cemetery he lies in is directly across the street from the house where our grandmother lived. Every time we sat down for Sunday lunches in Granny's dining room, my mother faced the window that looked out on her son's grave, that unmarked patch of grass amidst the acres of granite headstones. When my father went across the street to visit his mother's gravesite, he sometimes took us along to remember our brother. My mother never went. As my father bowed his head to say a silent prayer, I stood well back from the spot where Geoffrey lay. For some reason the earth had subsided slightly over the grave, and I had the notion that I would fall through that depression into a bottomless hole and be lost down there in the darkness with him forever.

Just a couple of years after Geoffrey's death, fate dealt our parents yet another cruel blow. A major car accident in the spring of 1952 was a calamity that very nearly caused them to lose another child. Though I don't know the exact date, I remember the accident very well. Mother had decided to learn how to drive and Dad was giving her a lesson with a car full of children. Mother was in the driver's seat of our blue Pontiac, Dad in the passenger seat with eighteen month old Jonnie in his lap, Bev and me in the back seat. Luckily, Greg was in school. Somehow Mother lost control, veered off the road, and plowed the car into a tree. Our parents both got nasty gashes in their foreheads from hitting the windshield. Bev and I were both unhurt except for a few bruises. But Jonnie suffered a fractured skull when her head hit a knob on the radio as she was catapulted forward.

I vividly recall the ride to the hospital in the ambulance. I was terrified as I sat in the front seat on a policeman's lap. I can still feel the rough wool of this jacket against my cheek as I laid my head on his chest. My parents sat behind me, bleeding profusely from the cuts on their heads. Jonnie and Bev were in the back with the attendants. The siren was wailing, traffic parting to let us through as we sped to the emergency room.

At the hospital Jonnie underwent emergency brain surgery, a risky experimental procedure with little chance of success. Miraculously, she defied the odds and not only survived, but showed no signs of brain

36

damage. Unknown to anyone at the time, however, there was hidden damage that later surfaced as dizzy spells throughout her childhood and eventually caused a seizure disorder in adulthood. For weeks after the accident she went through a long, nerve wracking recovery as she toddled around the house with a huge incision in her tender skull. Along with a wrecked car and huge hospital bills to worry about, our parents lived every day with fear for their seriously injured baby girl. As if the decision about the right course for Bev's future wasn't enough to handle, our parents now had to deal with the aftermath of this tragic automobile accident and the trauma of a close brush with death. For the Miller family, the light at the end of the tunnel was nowhere in sight.

Under very difficult circumstances, our parents did the best they could for Bev. How amidst all their troubles, with no money and no resources, could they keep Bev at home? Though they hated to send her away, they both truly believed that Bev was going to get an education at Pennhurst. It was, after all, called Pennhurst State *School*, and claimed to have special programs for teaching mentally retarded children. Bev had potential. Surely she could learn to do something useful that could assure her some sort of future in society? Surely the staff at Pennhurst knew what they were doing? Surely the doctors and psychologists knew what was best? Though I doubt that our parents were ever truly convinced, they eventually gave in to pressure, hoping that maybe everyone else was right. Perhaps one of the reasons our father didn't sign the admission papers was that he could not commit to the decision. Instead, he placed the responsibility on my mother to do the terrible deed. Maybe he felt less guilty through the years for not having put his name to that fateful document.

In the end our parents reluctantly sent their beautiful, troubled little girl to Pennhurst State School. It was the worst decision of their lives, one they regretted a thousand times over. I saw it in their eyes myriad times. When I was younger, I thought that look was sadness. Now that I am older I know that it was so much more. As Bev deteriorated month by month, then year by year, all hope vanished. The child they knew disappeared. The girl named Bev who lived at Pennhurst was no longer their child, but rather a creation of the institution. They had watched her fall down the rabbit hole, but unlike Alice, she took up permanent residence in a bizarre and bewildering world from which there was no return.

~4~

The Missing "E"

During the course of my investigations into Bev's life I came upon a startling fact. Not one official document I found in my research spelled her name the right way. My sister's name should be spelled not "Beverly" but "Beverley". Even though I had her birth certificate in my possession, I hadn't even noticed the spelling until I was researching our mother's correspondence with the Pennhurst State Hospital. I realized that Mother consistently spelled Bev's name with an "ey" rather than a "y". That prompted me to go back to look at the birth certificate and, sure enough, there was the name "Beverley". When I made this discovery I was both shocked and dismayed. First I was shocked that I didn't even know how to spell my own sister's name. My younger sister Jonnie and my brother Greg also had no idea. How could we go our whole lives not knowing such a simple fact? Yet more upsetting is the fact that our mother allowed Bev's name to be changed somewhere along the line. When did people first start misspelling her name and why didn't Mother correct it? This simple typographical error, allowed to continue uncorrected for the rest of Bev's life, speaks volumes about what happened to her. For me the missing "e" represents Bev's fate, summed up in the loss of one single letter. As soon as the system took possession of her, she lost her identity. She became what it made her. When the "e" disappeared, the real Beverley disappeared. How could she be saved when even her true name was lost?

BOOK TWO

1952 - 1983

Day After Day

It is never quiet. The air rings with a constant cacophony of screaming, crying, moaning, wailing, banging, babbling. Even at night, when everyone should be deep in sleep, there are nocturnal sounds - someone having a nightmare, a fuss in the bathroom, a conversation with faces in the dark. There is always movement. All day long there are swarms of people pacing, twisting, jerking, punching, rocking, gesturing to the empty air. The suffocating air stinks. There is the permeating odor of disinfectant over vomit, urine, feces, dirty diapers, spilled food and drink. There is no way to escape the chaos unless you are being punished and put in isolation. There are too many faces, too many hands, too many voices. Everyone is a stranger. This is not home. A sensitive, shy, intellectually disabled little girl with separation anxiety has come to live here. This is her life, day after day.

~5~

Welcome to Pennhurst

Beverley arrived at the Pennhurst State School at 3:30 PM on June 11, 1952, just two days after her ninth birthday. The original date of admission had been postponed from March 12 until June 11 because of a measles quarantine on the campus. These quarantines were not unusual because, in the overcrowded conditions there, communicable diseases spread rapidly throughout the population. In those days, of course, there were no vaccines for common childhood diseases like measles and chicken pox, and most children contracted them as a matter of course. As a result of the quarantine, her admission to Pennhurst became a misbegotten birthday gift. In addition to the bad timing, it seems appropriate that her name was misspelled on her admission papers, since after this date she became another person. The familiar Beverley who lived in an ordinary house, played with her brother and sisters, and was loved and cared for despite her disabilities, now became Beverly, case number 7525, imbecile.

That first day at Pennhurst was a frightening blur of events for Bev. After about an hour's car ride from home, she was driven through the gates of a huge hospital complex with acres of imposing brick buildings. The scene would have unfolded like a page out of Dickens. After the car finally pulled up at the door, she was led by her parents through the heavy doors of a cavernous turn of the century building to a polished wooden admissions desk where papers were solemnly signed. Then, after tearful hugs and kisses from Mom and Dad, she was handed over to white coated attendants, who pulled her, crying and struggling, down a long hallway into a tiled netherworld ruled by doctors and inhabited by dozens of other forlorn children.

Almost immediately, she was given a bath and evaluated by a nurse in the cottage she was assigned to. The notes say that she was biting and crying when she was first brought in, but calmed down later. In a report as antiseptic as the nurse's office, she was described as clean and well nourished with short brown curly hair, no vermin. Her personal effects were inventoried and recorded: one pair of panties, one dress, one pair of sandals, one pair of socks, one slip, a pair of eyeglasses and two rings After being bathed, examined, and fed, she was whisked off to a crowded dormitory. Still in shock, she was tucked into a strange bed in a room filled with other beds, other children, other nightmares. She was already terrified, yet the worst was yet to come. This little girl, who couldn't bear to be separated from her mother long enough even to attend kindergarten for a few hours, would be left to cope without her for days, weeks, months on end. What was to become of her?

Ten days later, after she had settled down enough to be evaluated, she was given a full physical and neurological examination. Physically she was deemed normal. Neurologically, with an IQ somewhere around 45, she was classified as an imbecile and recommended for occupational therapy. The report says that she bites her hands and forearms when she is displeased and screams often. The doctor diagnosed her as "no psychosis - mental deficiency". This is a significant point. When Bev entered Pennhurst her problems were primarily developmental and emotional. She was undoubtedly intellectually disabled and emotionally fragile, but at that time she exhibited no psychotic behavior. It was only after spending years at Pennhurst that she developed a range of psychological disorders which were actually brought on by the conditions of her confinement Pennhurst itself became her disease.

~6~

Decline and Fall

After Bev became a resident of Pennhurst State School, our family changed forever. She was still a daughter and sister in the Miller family, but she was no longer part of our day to day home life. Our daily routines went on without her, and the gaps left by her departure were quickly filled. For us children, though Bev may have been sorely missed at first, I don't believe it really took much time for us to learn to be without her. Children are resilient. They accept what happens to them when they are young because they don't know anything else. It takes a long time for them to find out about what goes on in the rest of the world. We didn't understand that our situation was unusual. So it was that, once Bev went away and we became intimately acquainted with the world of Pennhurst, we accepted it. We had no idea that most people would never see such a place, or even know that such a place existed. For us, however, it was a powerful childhood lesson. We found out at an early age that nightmares are real and some people live them every day. We thought it was normal.

Our family had suffered loss before when baby Geoffrey passed away. But Bev's departure was different. When Geoffrey died, he was gone. We imagined him in heaven, a sweet soul with feathery wings, living with the angels. But Bev was not in heaven. She was in school, but she didn't come home like Greg did every afternoon. She stayed at school forever and ever. Sometimes she came home for awhile, but she always went away again. While she was gone, we could forget about it, but each time she came home for a visit, we were reminded of how temporary she was. It was confusing. It didn't feel right.

Once Bev took up residence at Pennhurst, it was recommended that she not have contact with her family for a few weeks so that she could become acclimated to the institution. The first record of a visit is a letter from Mother requesting a vacation at home from September 11 to September 12, 1952, so that Bev could go to the Reading Fair. Bev loved going to the fair, and it would be a special treat for her. This was three months after Bev first walked through the doors of Pennhurst. The letter itself is very revealing. The tone is very polite and respectful and reveals an attitude of submission. The letter shows clearly that Mother has given over her parental rights to the institution and feels that they are in total control. Instead of insisting on her rights, she acts as though she no longer has any, that Pennhurst has taken over and she is at their mercy. Indeed, that was the prevailing policy in those days. Parents were expected to bow to the authority of the institution. Unfortunately, when dealing with a place like Pennhurst, a more assertive attitude would have been more appropriate, because without someone to protect her, Bev was bound to get swallowed up in the system.

Whenever our parents wanted their daughter to stay at home for more than one day, Mother needed to write a letter to request permission for a specific number of days. She generally requested extended visits in September to take Bev to the Reading Fair, in December for Christmas, and in June for her birthday. These were called Bev's "vacations." In between these extended stays were other holiday visits such as Thanksgiving and Easter. Most of the correspondence from these early months revolves around the visit requests or lists of personal items, like clothing and shoes, that Bev needed. It was only later that the letters started to take on a more ominous tone.

In the beginning having Bev at Pennhurst seemed to be a good solution to our parents' need to get help for her. They believed that having Bev there was like sending her off to a boarding school for children with special needs. After all, it was called Pennhurst State School, and it appeared to have the means to be able to educate her and to teach her how to behave like a "normal" child. Although she wasn't living at home, our parents were able to arrange visits so that she could still feel part of the family, especially for those special occasions like birthdays and Christmas. Not only did it appear that Bev was going to be better off, but now there was peace at home for the rest of us. Mother had more time to spend with her three other children, and more time to work outside the home and bring in much needed paychecks. It seemed that life was going to be better for everyone.

Though most of Mother's early correspondence with Pennhurst is about requests for home visits, some of these letters also request information about Bev's physical and mental condition and about her educational progress. The letters begin to show that not only was there no progress, but the longer Bev was at Pennhurst, the worse her overall condition became. As Bev's condition steadily deteriorated, Mother became increasingly upset with what was happening. A letter sent by Mother in August 1953, more than a year after Bev's admission, contains a long list of questions asking for very basic information that should have been made available far earlier. What had Bev been doing for the first year she was at Pennhurst? The reply letters seem to indicate that she hadn't been doing much of anything. Mother asks, "Does she receive any schooling at all?" Over a year after Bev's admission my parents didn't even know whether or not Bev was receiving any schooling! She also asks whether Bev has been tested lately, whether she receives medical treatment, how she is acclimating and getting along with other children, whether she attends church, and why she doesn't wear her eyeglasses. Mother also asks what Bev's day consists of and wants permission to come and observe Bev to see how she is living at Pennhurst. It is dismaying to realize that, over a year after her admission to Pennhurst, Bev's parents haven't a clue as to what is happening to their daughter.

The return letter from one of the doctors does not answer most of Mother's questions and does not issue an invitation for her to come and observe Bev's life in the institution. Whether or not our parents ever had a chance to make such a visit I don't know, but there is never any mention of it in letters or records. Records do show that Bev was tested in May 1953 and the results were about the same as when she was tested on admission in June 1952. The doctor states that Bev is not a candidate for a formal classroom and recommends that she be tried in Occupational Therapy. In his reply to Mother, the doctor talks only about the testing and the recommendation for Occupational Therapy. Her other questions go unanswered. Again, in December 1953, when Mother writes to request Bev's Christmas vacation, she asks for a report on her progress and is told only that Bev is "enjoying good health." Despite their inquiries, our parents remain uninformed, and Bev continues to languish for yet another year until circumstances take an alarming turn for the worse late in 1954.

There are very few letters for the entire year of 1954 until the month of December. Whether or not they went missing or never existed, I don't know, but I believe that there may not have been any, because this year turned out to be one of dramatic changes for our family. Our parents' financial problems finally came to a head and resulted in a declaration of bankruptcy sometime in 1954. The bank stepped in and took our house and everything in it, except for our personal possessions. Even some of those disappeared as Dad sold as many of our meager possessions as he could, including many of our toys, in order to scrape up enough money for us to move elsewhere and pay the first month's rent. I stood by bewildered as one of our neighbors from down the street came into our house and carried away the toy upright piano I had gotten for Christmas. In the end we left our home with not much more than the clothes on our backs. During this time of upheaval, it is doubtful that Bev would have been visiting us at home, and our parents probably had less time even to visit her at Pennhurst. Though it was customary for her to have vacations at home for her birthday and the Reading Fair, there were no written requests for those visits this year. The first recorded request for an extended visit was for her Christmas vacation in December. This is when the correspondence began to indicate real problems with Bev's behavior.

A letter from Pennhurst on December 2, 1954 informs our parents that Bev will be tried in a "Training Program" starting in January of 1955. This training program, which had previously excluded Bev, had been expanded to include trainable as well as educable patients. When Mother's return letter asks for details about the classes, she is told to write again in February to find out how Bev was doing after she had been in the program for a few weeks. Oddly this decision to put Bev in a training class was made when her behavior had begun deteriorating rather than improving. However, our parents knew nothing about her escalating behavior problems until they took Bev home for her annual

Christmas vacation. A letter written by Mother after the visit expresses shock at Bev's appearance. Her hair had been cut so short that she was nearly bald. This was the beginning of a long period of time when her hair was clipped in order to keep her from pulling it. Unbeknownst to our parents, this behavior had been going on for several weeks before her Christmas visit.

When Superintendent Phillips received Mother's emotional letter, he requested an explanation of the situation from the Assistant Director of Nurses in the Female Colony. Her report explains that Bev had begun pulling out her hair during her "disturbed periods". The doctor in charge of the Female Colony then ordered that Bev be placed in a "camisole" to prevent her from pulling her hair. Our parents had never been informed about these disturbed periods or the use of a camisole to restrain Bev. When the superintendent answered Mother's letter to explain why Bev's hair was cut, he did mention the use of a camisole, but it wasn't until over four months later that Mother asked for an explanation of what that actually meant.

In a reply letter, the doctor in charge of the Female Colony, finally gives Mother information she should have received months earlier. He describes a camisole as "a jacket of a light canvas material which envelops the upper part of the body and confines the hands so that the child is unable to inflict harm to herself or others". He is describing what would more commonly be called a straight jacket. The fact that he refers to it with a quaint name like camisole doesn't change its purpose. It was used to tie Bev's arms down so that she couldn't pull at her hair. By the time the doctor told Mother about it, he had already been using the straightjacket on Bev for three months. Clinical Progress Reports show that Bev had been restrained in a camisole during the month of December 1954 on 25 days, and almost EVERY DAY during the following months of January and February! An eleven year old child had been placed in a straight jacket nearly every day for over three months because she pulled her hair. Unknowingly, by complaining about Bev's short hair, Mother may have condemned Bev to this treatment, because it was the only way Pennhurst staff could let her hair grow out.

Apparently restraining Bev wasn't very effective, because by March of 1955 the doctor seems to have given up on using the camisole. Instead, Bev was "reclassified" and moved from Cottage 3 to Cottage 4, which was for more disturbed children. After the move, her hair was cut off again. When Aunt Ruth visited her in April, she was upset by Bev's appearance and told our parents about it. That visit prompted Mother to write another letter in which she complained about Bev's hair and finally asked what a camisole is. In that same letter she also asks about Bev's progress in school. Of course, since she didn't know about Bev's extreme behavior problems, she couldn't know that Bev wasn't even attending school, let alone making any progress.

In his reply to Mother, the doctor does inform her that Bev was taken out of the Training Program because she is, "destructive, frequently soils herself in class, and pulls out her hair." Mother's hopes for progress were certainly dashed by these developments. There is no written response from her as to the shocking information in the doctor's letter. What response she may have made by phone or in person I don't know, because there is no further written correspondence on record until September. These letters in early 1955 show that Bev obviously had gone into a sharp decline beginning late in 1954. It is heartbreaking to read Mother's repeated pleas for information about her daughter's imagined progress. Mother kept expecting to hear positive reports about Bev's educational development. She honestly believed that Bev was receiving schooling. Her letters frequently ask if there has been any change in Bev's I.Q. By June of 1954 Bev had been in Pennhurst for two years, yet during this time not much had been done to give Bev any kind of education. Even after two years with no positive results, Mother still wanted to believe that Pennhurst was a school that was going to teach Beverley what she could not and that it was possible for her I.Q. to improve. Despite all her disappointments, she clung to her faith that Bev was going to get better.

Many factors had been coming together to push Bev steadily downhill. Besides the lack of educational opportunity at Pennhurst, living in the chaotic and impersonal atmosphere of the institution took a heavy toll. Bev desperately needed the security of her home. She craved her parents' attention, their hugs and kisses and their soothing reassurances when the world pressed in on her, filling her with fear. Unfortunately, during this year when they were going through their bankruptcy and household move, they had less time for her. The entire family was traumatized by the changes in our circumstances. No one was happy. When the move was completed, the home Bev recognized was gone. That familiar house was left behind, the house Bev always thought of as "home", the one with the proverbial white picket fence. It was the last house our parents ever owned and, once we left it, their dream of a secure and happy family life faded like the photographs they took there. To make matters worse, not only were Bev's surroundings unfamiliar, but her siblings were growing up and changing as well. The one thing she could always count on - home - had deserted her. Her familiar world was beginning to disintegrate.

The place we moved to after our parents' bankruptcy was a rented row house in the heart of the city of Reading. Since the bank had repossessed our house, we needed to find a cheap rental property in a hurry. Bev was eleven years old and had been living at Pennhurst for two years when we made that move. I was seven, Greg twelve, Jonnie four. Leaving our house in Mohnton was a traumatic event for all of us. Even though it was a place fraught with tragedy, it was our home and we were heartbroken to leave it. We felt like a band of gypsies as we piled into the car, our parents in the front seat and the three of us in the rear. We were squeezed tightly together, buried amongst piles of clothes and household items. In my lap I held the birdcage containing our frantic parakeet, who fluttered around spewing feathers and birdseed all over us. It was an uncomfortable, sombre ride, and our arrival at our new home did nothing to cheer us up.

The house was situated in the middle of a long row of attached homes on a very steep, narrow street with uneven brick sidewalks and slate curbs. As was the custom in the inner city, an alley lined with garbage cans and dog poop ran behind the houses to allow access to small garages. The yard was a tiny patch of scrub grass, sandwiched in between the house and the one car garage in the rear of the property. The inside of the house was dark and dingy, the furniture old and worn. The arrangement with the landlord was peculiar. It was her house, fully furnished with her things. For some reason she retained one of the bedrooms for herself, and although she didn't actually live there anymore, she often came and went unannounced. Since I was just a child, I didn't know the details of the arrangement, but I found it unnerving to have this strange lady appearing every now and then, moving silently past like ghost. I was afraid of her and was nervous when she was in the house.

Because the inner city neighborhood was not safe, an older neighbor girl walked me to and from the local elementary school a few blocks away. Unless she was with me, I was not allowed to venture out of the yard or off the covered front porch to play. Occasionally, as a treat, she would walk me to a playground which was on the far side of a busy street at the bottom of the hill. Her name was Susie, and she was my guardian angel. Her Roman Catholic family observed meatless Fridays, and sometimes had pancakes for their evening meal. When they did, Susie invited me to join them for what I felt was the best supper ever. As a result of being so sequestered, I had no playmates other than our immediate neighbors, two porcine children who were as mean as they were fat. I didn't like the neighborhood, I didn't like the kids, and I didn't like the school. I was in second grade at the time and had an unpleasant old teacher, with blue hair piled on top of her head like an eighteenth century wig. The teacher's pet was a pale blond girl who wore beautiful flouncy dresses to school every day. I didn't like her either. It was a lonely, dreary existence. We were all unhappy in that house, but we were desperate for a roof over our heads, and we had to make do.

Bev did not fare well during this period, either at Pennhurst or at home. There was very little time for our parents to spend with her while they were struggling to put food on the table, pay the bills, and look after their three other children. I was still too young to understand or remember much that was going on during those unfortunate times. I don't have any recollection of Bev coming to visit in that house. I doubt that she did. Luckily we didn't live in that creepy inner city house for long. In just over a year we moved yet again. Once our parents started to get back on their feet after their financial crisis, we moved to Sinking Spring, a little borough a few miles to the west of Reading, at the very last stop on the city bus line. That was in the summer of 1955. Although the move was a happy one for the rest of us children, it would have been yet another unwelcome change for Bev. Within three years of Bev's admission to Pennhurst we had already moved twice. Her life continued to unravel.

Our parents' financial difficulties had forced our family into a kind of peripatetic life as they found it necessary to leave one home after another. We were like nomads folding up our tents in the night to stay one step ahead of our creditors. Our brother Greg, the firstborn, wound up living in six different houses by the time he graduated from high school. After the bankruptcy our parents were never able to get credit again and couldn't afford to buy a house or a car or anything else that entailed borrowing money. After Mohnton, we always lived in rental properties, and Dad took sales jobs that provided him with a company car. By this time we knew the drill. New house, new neighborhood, new schools, new friends - again.

Sinking Spring turned out to be a great place for us kids. It was safe and clean and folksy, with lots of places to roam and play. There was a shady park with swings and pavilions, as well as a stream to wade in. It was called Socialist Park when we first arrived, but the name was changed soon after to Willow Glen, not surprising in the paranoid atmosphere of the fifties. At the very end of the park stood an old fashioned roller skating rink, with wooden floors and live organ music, where we spent many a fun-filled Saturday afternoon whizzing around in endless circles on our rented skates. Besides the park, there was also a large playground with swings and seesaws and a sandbox and a program of organized activities in the summertime. Every week there was an outdoor movie night where we lay on blankets under the stars to watch Laurel and Hardy, Martin and Lewis, or Hope and Crosby. There were quiet streets for bike riding and smooth sidewalks for roller skating and hopscotch. Behind our house lay an open field and a pine grove to roam around in. The Sinking Spring Elementary School, a twenty minute walk from our house, was a small neighborhood school with no nonsense old ladies in flowered dresses and orthopedic shoes staffing the classrooms.

Our house was a big, stone eighteenth century farmhouse, which had been divided in half to accommodate two families. The landlords and their children lived on one side, our family on the other. It could have been a beautiful house had it been refurbished and restored, but instead it was a rundown, drafty old place with few amenities. Actually the only amenities were hot and cold running water and electricity. Its primary appeal was incredibly cheap rent. Although it was very Spartan, we children loved it. After feeling like prisoners in the gloomy row house in Reading, we felt like birds released from a cage into our light airy house with its big, grassy front yard, neighborhood playmates just down the lane, and plenty of safe places to play.

The front door of the house entered into a huge kitchen, the floor a rectangular expanse of pale linoleum. When my parents weren't home, I sometimes took advantage of that tempting open space to roller skate around the room. The far end contained the appliances, the sink was midway along the outer wall, and the only furniture was a redwood picnic table at the near end by the door. A doorway led into the living room, a rectangle that paralleled the kitchen. Next to the doorway was an open space where the wall had been cut out to let more light into the living room. A birdcage usually hung there, housing a succession of blue parakeets, all named "Billy". The living room contained a television, an easy chair and a sofa, as well as a gas space heater at the end nearest the staircase. That space heater was the only heat for the entire house. In winter the upstairs was frigid, and we children huddled in our blankets as we came downstairs for breakfast. In the bathroom the toilet seat was so cold that my teeth chattered when I sat on it first thing after waking. To add to the chill, the windows let in icy drafts, despite the clear plastic covers that our landlord tacked on the outside. In wintertime I lay in my bed listening to the cold winds howling around the corner of the house, madly flapping the plastic outside our bedroom window all night long.

The staircase was an enclosed wooden spiral, typical of such old Pennsylvania German farmhouses. The fan shaped steps were treacherous for us children, and we tumbled down often. The stairs led to three bedrooms, two small ones in the back of the house and a large one over the kitchen. All the floors were covered with the omnipresent linoleum in various crazy quilt patterns. A tiny bathroom opened off our parents' bedroom. There were no doors on any of the rooms in the house and only a sliding plastic curtain to provide privacy for the bathroom. Since there were no closets, also typical for such old houses, our clothes were hung on portable metal racks or folded and stacked on the deep windowsills. Actually the landlord had fashioned a small wallboard closet in one corner of our parents' room, but there was no space in it for the children's clothes. On cold winter mornings I pulled on icy underwear plucked from the piles of clothes on the drafty window sill in our room.

Jonnie and I slept in the first small bedroom at the top of the stairs. There was room for only our two beds and a small table. The walls were painted a bright bluish green, which always reminded me of the interior of a swimming pool. At the foot of my bed was a door behind which another spiral staircase led to a large dusty attic. Many a night I woke with a start as I imagined that door opening slowly to let some fuzzy gremlin creep into my room. Greg slept in a smaller room which he could reach only by walking through ours. In it he had only a bed and a chest of drawers. When he was a teenager, he covered up the swimming pool green with red and white paint and drew bizarre cartoons, inspired by MAD Magazine, all over the walls.

As usual, our poor mother suffered the most from this house's inconveniences. It was a long bus ride for her to her place of employment at Western Electric, which was as far to the east of Reading as our house was to the west. She worked second shift at first and came home on the last bus at almost midnight. The walk from the bus stop up a rutted dirt road to the house was long and dark and spooky, freezing cold in winter. She was probably very thankful when she finally transferred to day shift and was able to carpool or have our father pick her up and bring her home. Since we had no washer or dryer, our washing needed to be dropped off at a commercial laundry, an expensive option that forced my mother to do smaller items by hand and hang them on a wash line in the yard. The lack of central heat, cold bare floors, minimal furniture, and no privacy certainly made her life uncomfortable. The spare kitchen with old appliances and almost no counter space or storage must have made feeding the family a chore. Although living there gave our parents a chance to save some money and get back on their feet, living on the cheap was no picnic for our mom.

There certainly were no frills in this house, but something more important was noticeably missing. There was no bedroom for Bev. This fact made it clear that she was never going to live with us again. By this time our parents obviously realized that Pennhurst was not just a boarding school where Bev would stay temporarily to get an education and improve her behavior. She would stay at Pennhurst for a very long time, perhaps forever. As far as we children were concerned, she might as well have been on the moon. Just as there was no place for her in this house, there was no place for her in the family anymore. The rest of us were moving on and leaving Bev far behind in Pennhurst.

Even though Bev was by that time firmly entrenched at Pennhurst, we still saw her fairly frequently and it is here that I remember most of Bev's home visits. The majority of Bev's time with us at home revolved around holidays or her birthday, though she also came for some time in the summer. Once my mother was working full time, Bev was able to come primarily just for weekends. A typical visit started when our parents pulled up in the driveway with Bev in the car. After she got out of the car she barreled across the lawn and burst through the front door wailing like a banshee. The moment she set foot in the door she started whining for candy and soda. She never said "hello" or even acknowledged our presence. She had her priorities, and the first one was food. We just stood back and stayed out of her way while Mother sat her down and gave her a lollipop or a few twists of licorice to settle her before unpacking her bag. Even if she wasn't staying overnight, Bev always arrived with a carryall stuffed with a change of clothes and her medications.

I always dreaded hearing the words, "Watch her", which my mother would say when she needed to leave Bev unattended for a few minutes. I held my breath hoping Bev wouldn't do anything terrible while I was temporarily in charge of her. If Bev got up to leave the room I yelled "Mom!" rather than try to restrain her. Bev needed help doing just about everything except eating. Going to the bathroom, brushing her teeth, getting dressed, all required someone's assistance. Poor mother barely got a moment's rest. It's not that Bev wasn't able to do those things, but at Pennhurst it was faster and easier for the attendants to do things for the residents than to wait for them to do them on their own. Many times they didn't get them done at all. As a result, the residents became more and more helpless instead of more independent.

We didn't do anything special when she visited. We mostly stayed in and around the house, though we occasionally want to see our grandmother, Aunt Ruth and Uncle Bill, or Aunt Florence. We tried to keep her time with us quiet and uncomplicated so that she would remain calm. Since Bev's favorite activity was eating, mealtimes and snacks were very important to her. Birthdays always included lots of cake and ice cream, of course, while the holidays revolved around cookies and candy. Food was also always a reliable way to appease her and keep her subdued. As a result, during these years she gained a great deal of weight. She ate far too much, both at Pennhurst and at home.

It was difficult to take Bev on any sort of excursion because of her unpredictable behavior. She often became agitated and continually engaged in compulsive movements like rocking, pulling her hair, twirling around like a whirling dervish or playing with her fingers. She had a habit of whining loudly when she was tired or hungry or upset. Any sort of noise or commotion could cause a tantrum. The possibility of an outburst at anytime created a high level of tension for everyone. Our parents were able to settle her down eventually, but there was always the possibility that one day she might get completely out of control and we would be helpless to deal with it.

We siblings didn't know what to do with her at home. She couldn't play with us without becoming combative. Almost everything we did upset her. We never knew what would set off a bout of whining and crying and hitting. Her mood swings were unpredictable, true for any teenager but even more so for Bev, and she could become quite violent when angry. It was a rare visit when one of us didn't get slugged or pushed when she was upset about something. When she ate her meals she gobbled her food as fast as possible and guarded her plate against any perceived attempts to steal what was on it. She moved ungracefully and plowed into anyone who got in her way. She regarded any physical touch as a potential assault and defended herself unnecessarily against even accidental contact. The only ones who could safely approach her were her mom and dad.

When she was visiting, Mother's time was taken up completely with managing her, and our role was mainly to stay out of the way. We were happy to oblige. During the five and a half years we lived in Sinking Spring, Bev was between the ages of twelve and seventeen, her crucial adolescence. Unfortunately, as she grew from child to young woman, she became more difficult for our parents to handle. The staff at Pennhurst used restraints, isolation, and drugs to control her outbursts. At home, of course, it was a different story. Bev loved her parents and tried to be good for them, but eventually her erratic behavior was more than they could handle on their own, and the Christmas of 1956 was the last vacation that Bev had at home. After that, because the doctors at Pennhurst strongly advised against extended visitations, we began seeing Bev more frequently at Pennhurst rather than bringing her home for visits.

During our time in Sinking Spring, our parents were still struggling financially as they tried to recover from their bankruptcy. It was a slow process, and our lifestyle was bare bones. Times were tough, but at least we had hope. Mother got a good job at the Western Electric plant with a steady paycheck that allowed our parents to pay at least most of the bills. Dad, still working as a salesman, continued to change jobs frequently, but was bringing in good money when he did work. It was a "steak or beans" existence, but there was always food on the table and the rent got paid more or less on time. However, despite the fact our mother's new job provided a steady paycheck, financial problems continued to dog them, and there never seemed to be enough money for more than the bare essentials. Financial responsibility was not our father's strong suit. Any extra money in his pocket was quickly spent.

Our parents argued frequently, small disagreements at the dinner table or in the car, and more dramatic altercations late at night when they thought their children were asleep. Although I didn't catch on until later, another reason for the arguments, besides money, was our father's infidelities. In his job as a salesman, he met a lot of people including, apparently, a lot of willing ladies. Many evenings he went out after supper to keep a sales appointment and didn't come home until very late. It took me a long time to realize that he couldn't be working until ten or eleven o'clock at night. Many of his appointments were after business hours, and many of his meetings took place in bars. For the most part we children were unaware of the depth of the conflict. On the surface all seemed well and the arguing didn't seem worse than what went on in a lot of other families.

During the time that Jonnie and I were too young to be left at home on our own in the evenings while Mother worked second shift, Dad had to take us along with him on some of his sales calls. We hated being left in the car for what seemed like hours while Dad was inside someone's house trying to sell whatever was his current wonder product. Sitting together in the dark car was both scary and boring. We passed the time playing word games or singing songs or just gazing out the window hoping to see Dad returning before our bladders burst. Afterwards, he often took us with him to one of his favorite watering holes to have either a celebratory or consolation drink. He parked Jonnie and me in a back booth to sip CocaCola, while he sat at the bar to have his shot and a beer and make boozy conversation with the local patrons. I grew to hate those dimly lit barrooms with their smell of musty carpets and cigarette butts and alcohol and, in the background, just the faintest tinge of vomit. If Dad happened to have some pocket change, we could play with the jukebox to pass the time with Elvis or Sinatra while we waited for him to be lubricated enough to go home. No one was happier than we were when Mother started working the day shift.

Meanwhile, much of the time, there was a lot of fun and laughter and a general feeling of well being. Jonnie and I were happy at school and church. We had close friends in the neighborhood and spent many hours with them playing and exploring and growing up together. Greg was an offbeat teenager who hung out with his buddies or puttered around in his room, drawing or fooling around with cameras or telescopes or crazy experiments. Even though I could appreciate why he lived in his own world and avoided a lot of the family drama, I always wished that he would spend more time with us. Yet, despite all our hardships, life was good. We could even say we were happy. The Miller family was no longer down and out, but up and coming.

Probably the most important positive influence on our lives while we lived in Sinking Spring was our church. We attended a Lutheran church in downtown Reading, a very conservative congregation with a strong German influence. The pastor was of German heritage, spoke German fluently, and conducted a high German church service once a month. Since the services, including the German one, were broadcast on the radio, parishioners like our Aunt Florence, who rarely left her house, could listen at home. Our glamorous Aunt Ruth attended occasionally, showing up at the services in her Sunday finery, including fancy hats with delicate veils and a full length fur coat that awed Jonnie and me. It seemed that all the people most important to our dad were part of this church in some way. We were very involved in church life, and it had a very positive effect on us as a family. Dad was an unofficial deacon, Mother was in the Ladies' Guild, Jonnie and I attended Sunday School classes and sang in the choir, Greg was an acolyte. It was here that Greg first entertained thoughts of being a minister someday. It was a huge part of the fabric of our family during those years.

Since Mother had few friends and rarely went anywhere except with her husband or her children, the church provided her with an opportunity to be with other women and to do something for herself. As a member of the Ladies' Guild she participated in group activities and began to bloom. The church also sponsored occasional bus trips to places like New York City or Washington, D.C., and Mother, Jonnie, and I often went on the excursions. Since our family never went anywhere more exciting than an amusement park, these trips were eye opening experiences for us. They expanded our horizons and gave the three of us an enticing taste of independence.

The church was also a stabilizing influence on our father. All his life he struggled with inner demons that stemmed, in large part, from his being abandoned by his father when he was a young boy. He was an insecure man who sabotaged his happiness with self destructive behaviors he couldn't control. As a result, his family became his emotional punching bag. When he was up, he was mischievous and fun to be with. He took us for rides in the countryside, sat through Disney movies with us at drive in theaters, bought us ice cream cones, and drove us to the park to feed the ducks. When he was down, he could be cruel, berating us, calling us names, and blaming us for all his troubles. When he was drunk, he was dangerous. He drove like a madman even with his children in the car. He left us home alone or locked us in the car while he went for a drink. Alcohol became his substitute for psychotherapy, and the church became his refuge. For many years, it was able to help him cope. Unfortunately, it wasn't enough.

Greg loved the church and found, in religion, comfort and sense of purpose. He became friends with our pastor, served faithfully as an acolyte, and seriously considered going into the ministry even as a teenager. It would be many years before he fulfilled that dream, but that church provided his first real spiritual home and inspiration for his future life. Greg, Jonnie and I all felt secure in the church. It was the one place where nothing bad could happen.

It was within this church that my parents were the most open about Bev, and I believe that they had support from both the pastor and fellow congregants to help them cope with their situation. Coincidentally, there was also another family in the church that had a daughter about the same age as Bev with similar disabilities. The big difference was, that while Bev was in Pennhurst, the other girl was living at home with her parents and siblings. She was even able to come with the family to church, whereas Bev did not. This was the first time Jonnie and I had met someone like Bev outside Pennhurst, and I wondered why it was that this girl was able to live at home while Bev had to be sent away. I never discussed it with my parents, and I couldn't seem to resolve it in my own mind. I am sure that there were must have been very good reasons, but getting to know this family planted the first seeds of doubt about Pennhurst in my mind. It was the first time I began to wonder "why?"

Knowing this girl's family gave our mother some idea of what it would have been like to have kept Bev at home. I never actually heard Mother talk about regretting the decision to send Bev to Pennhurst, but through the years it was painfully clear to me that she did regret it and, had she known the outcome, would never have placed her daughter there. The presence of both our families in the church was a constant reminder of the isolation that parents with mentally handicapped children experienced in those days. A church would have been one of the only places to provide any support. Making the decision to keep a child like Bev at home was not an easy one, and parents who did so experienced a lifetime of both financial and personal struggle. There were few social services or education options for people trying to cope with taking care of children with special needs. For families without money there were only two choices. Either you struggled at home on your own, with almost no help from outside sources, or you placed your child in a state-run institution like Pennhurst.

There is no doubt that, instead of being Bev's salvation, Pennhurst proved to be her undoing. Bev's original problems stemmed from mental retardation and a low I.Q. that made comprehension and learning difficult for her. Her emotional outbursts were fueled by her frustration at living in a world she couldn't understand. Her fear and anxiety made her emotionally immature and insecure. She was a child who needed specialized instruction in order to learn and constant positive reinforcement to keep her emotionally stable so that she could learn. Today's special education teachers would have the tools and skills to help Bev. Unfortunately in the 1950's this wasn't the case, and a child like Bev had no opportunity to develop what intellectual abilities she had.

It is particularly hard to look at what happened to our sister in light of today's standards. Bev was simply born in the wrong place at the wrong time. First of all she was born into a family that didn't have the financial means to care for her properly. In those days, the only place to get help would have been a private clinic, hospital, or school that would have cost a great deal of money. Bev wound up in Pennhurst because her family was poor and the state hospital was all they could afford. However, even if our parents had been wealthier, the care available at that time was still more custodial than educational. She would have had nicer surroundings and more personal attention, but she still would not have progressed much in her capacity to deal with the world or to find a productive place in it.

The truth of the matter is that Bev had real potential for development. With her emotional issues under control, she could have learned many skills. Progress would have been slow, but it could have happened. The tragedy is, that in the 1950's, it would not. Not for Bev, not for anyone. Today she might be diagnosed with autism, obsessive/compulsive disorder, attention deficit disorder, Tourette Syndrome, and other widely recognized conditions. In a modern setting, even the average elementary classroom teacher would have a good idea of what was going on with Bev. Her disabilities would have been evident and there would be methods to deal with them. Educational opportunities would be readily available. Unfortunately for Bev, babies born during World War II didn't have much chance for successful treatment. They would have to wait for better times. It would be over twenty years before mental health issues received much recognition, and nearly thirty years before long-overdue reforms touched Beverley's life. With proper medication and adaptive teaching techniques, who knows what Bev could have become? What she did become was a ghost, wandering the halls of an institution that didn't know what to do with beautiful little girls with dark brown eyes and the "inability to conform".

When Bev first entered Pennhurst she was an emotionally unstable little girl with pronounced mental retardation. After a year and a half in that institution she completed her fall down the rabbit hole into a distorted world of complete madness. Even the most well adjusted individual would have had difficulty maintaining her sanity in conditions like those at Pennhurst. For awhile, Bev was able to keep a grip on reality, but after her continued exposure to institutional life and the loss of the home life that she desperately needed, she entered into a realm of isolation where her only companions were the demons that tormented her.

The Beverley we knew, the shy and gentle young girl with the soft brown eyes, had finally disappeared.

~7~

Lost in a Desert World

In 1994, a slim memoir called *Lost in a Desert World* was published, not long after the death of its author Roland Johnson, who was a former disabled resident of Pennhurst State School and Hospital. It is the story of his experiences at Pennhurst as told to a writer named Karl Williams. Roland Johnson was an extraordinary individual who was sent to Pennhurst in 1958 at the age of twelve and lived there for ten years. When he was released from Pennhurst and began living in the community, he became an advocate for the rights of citizens with intellectual disabilities and eventually became president of a group called "Speaking for Ourselves", based in Philadelphia, PA. Roland had an outstanding career with this group, traveling both in the U.S. and abroad to talk to both mental health professionals and people with developmental disabilities, advocating for more independence and self determination for the disabled. As the leader of this group, he became the voice for hundreds of disenfranchised men and women like Bev who could not speak for themselves. He also became an inspiration for so many people who saw what a man, once incarcerated and abused, could accomplish when given the opportunity to reach the height of his intellectual abilities. When he died in 1994 at the age of only 49, he left behind a legacy of personal triumph and public advocacy for the rights of the intellectually challenged. Part of that legacy is his book *Lost in a Desert World*.

Roland was sent to Pennhurst at the age of twelve when his erratic behavior became too much for his parents to handle. Although intellectually challenged, he was able to attend school and became one of the higher functioning residents. Eventually, he became one of the working inmates at the institution. A great deal of the menial labor at Pennhurst was actually done by residents like him, under the supervision of paid staff. Those who were farmhands looked after animals and planted and harvested the crops. The indoor workers performed housecleaning tasks and mopped up messes, worked in the dining hall and kitchens, did laundry, and ran errands. Many of them were also called upon to assist with the personal care of the lower functioning individuals. Roland even learned how to give haircuts. It was these "volunteer" workers who made it possible for Pennhurst to function with inadequate staff and insufficient funding. In the last three decades of its existence, when the patient population was being reduced, the need for staff actually increased because of the loss of these unpaid resident workers. Roland was one of the most capable and was able to move freely around the buildings and grounds. Because of his relative freedom and familiarity with staff, he was able to see what was going on behind the scenes, and he had the intellectual capacity to report on it.

Since Bev lived at Pennhurst from 1952 until 1984, Roland was there at the same time she was. The world that Roland describes so vividly in his book was also Bev's world, but he had the ability to tell us what Bev never could. When I read Roland's account I learned so much about what Bev lived through for 32 years but could never put into words. Her comments were limited to repetitive phrases such as "I don't like the day room", "she hit me", "pull my teeth out", "she's bad", "I don't want to go back", "no movies tonight", "I'll be good". Most of our knowledge of Pennhurst was limited to our brief experiences when we visited Bev there. Of course we could hear the screaming and smell the noxious odors coming through the windows, but we had only a superficial view of hallways and reception areas and the grounds. We had no idea what went on behind the facade. Roland fills in the blanks, and they are not pretty.

He begins his account by describing his arrival at Pennhurst at the age of twelve, how frightening it was being driven down the long road, past the water tower, and onto the vast grounds. Bev was just nine, and just as terrified, when she took that same drive six years earlier. The first stop was the hospital, where new patients were bathed and evaluated both physically and mentally. They remained there for several days before being put on the appropriate ward according to their level of disability. The wards were crowded rooms with long rows of beds on each side. Each patient was given a locker to keep his or her few personal belongings. Females and males lived in separate cottages, and in each cottage was a day room where residents spent their time when not on their wards. These were bare rooms with little furniture, usually just some benches and a television mounted on the wall. People either sat rocking or staring into space or wandering around aimlessly muttering to themselves or wailing or picking fights. As Roland describes it, "It sounded like vibrations: crazy people was going out of their heads, out of their wits…It was just scary - a frightened, scary place."

The patients at Pennhurst ranged from severely developmentally delayed, many with physical handicaps as well, to merely learning disabled. While Roland was a high functioning individual, Bev was what he refers to as a "low grade." The low grade wards were the worst. That is where Bev lived. Roland paints a dismal picture of these wards. "To tell you the truth, Pennhurst smelled like a dog house. It just smell like feces. Rats crawling, roaches crawling all over; this was on the low grade wards. Holes in the wall, big holes in the floors. It was awful to see. You would cry to see people living in that kind of filth."

I personally remember that well, the smell of the place. It would cling to Bev like a second skin. As youngsters, when we visited her, we didn't like to get too near. Her hygiene wasn't good, she wore no deodorant, and the odor of the wards was embedded in her clothes. We could barely stand it for an hour. She lived with it 24 hours a day. In another passage Roland describes the protective screens that I remember seeing over the windows when we visited. They were kept locked to prevent the patients from pushing them open to break the glass or jump out. They blocked much of the light from outdoors and made it difficult to see out. In the summer heat, the windows were opened behind the screens, allowing both the pitiful wailing and the suffocating odors to waft outside.

The horrible living conditions fostered an atmosphere of violence and abuse, which Roland describes in detail. The residents sometimes fought among themselves and caused injuries to each other, mostly lacerations and bruises. Sometimes, though, they were injured by attendants. Most of this physical abuse was not done out of malice, but desperation. When attendants were assigned to watch large groups of patients they often resorted to force to subdue someone who was out of control. For them it was often a matter of personal survival, or a desperate way to protect innocent bystanders from being hurt in a melee. There were too few staff, and many of the staff were poorly trained and poorly equipped to handle the pressures caused by overcrowding and lack of meaningful activity for bored residents. It was an explosive situation.

Besides physical assault, there were also sexual assaults. Sexual abuse did occur, both patient on patient and attendant on patient. Roland talks about his own sexual abuse at the hands of older male residents, and he describes incidents that occurred to others, including one that ended in a murder that prompted a State Police investigation. As far as Bev goes, I know for a fact that she suffered physical abuse because I saw the cuts and bruises and bite marks on her every time we visited. Some were self inflicted, many were not. Whether she suffered sexual abuse, I can't say for sure. There is no proof, and she can't tell us. Roland's memory, however, is clear.

> I got scared at around the nighttime. All this stuff happened late at night. Lot of people was sleeping. And they'd be boys with these grown people and they would be waking up other people, their friends, getting them out of bed. I thought that they was going to do that to me. And they did and I couldn't do nothing about it. At that time I was sexual abused.

Amazingly, Roland also has some happy memories and tells about some of the good things that happened to him while he was at Pennhurst. He was able to attend school, where he felt safe and protected by the teachers. He was able to go to the playground, play baseball, and belong to the Boy Scouts. He went to church. He describes picnics and Easter egg hunts and Santa Claus. Because he was a higher functioning individual he was able to participate in all of these activities. In her early years at Pennhurst Bev had fewer of these experiences because of her more severe retardation. Her records show that she attended school only briefly because of her uncooperative and belligerent behavior. Unfortunately, these behaviors kept her from participating in many of the activities that would have enhanced her life there. She spent more time being restrained and punished than having fun. The rare picnic or a visit from Santa were brief respite from a daily life of boredom and despair. While Bev was confined within the walls of Pennhurst, I never saw her smile. Never.

Roland Johnson was officially discharged from Pennhurst in 1971 at the age of 26, after successfully transitioning to a group home. He was one of the first residents to be able to take advantage of the Community Living Arrangements that began to be implemented after the passage of the Pennsylvania Mental Health and Retardation Act of 1966. Bev remained at Pennhurst until 1984. By then she was was 41 years old, the prime of her life left far behind. Conditions there continued to improve from the mid sixties until she finally was released into the community, but her precious youth was spent suffering through the circumstances that Roland described in his personal account. Like him, she, too, was lost in a desert world.

~8~

Wonderland

Visitors. That's what we became after June 11, 1952 when our only interaction with Bev was during some sort of visitation, either at home or at Pennhurst. The nature and frequency of these visits evolved as Bev got older, her condition got worse, and our family dynamic changed. When Bev first went away at the age of nine, visits were special occasions. We all looked forward to seeing her and having a good time. Our parents and other relatives bought gifts and clothes and candy and tried to create a festive atmosphere. Everyone was hoping, as well, to see improvement in Bev's behavior and intellectual development. The first visits were full of optimism and happiness, but where they had once been anticipated as joyous occasions, they gradually became sad and disheartening experiences that grew worse as time went on.

Once the initial restrictions on visits were lifted and she was finally allowed to come home in those first two years, Bev came not just for day visits, but for "vacations" which lasted for as long as a week. She soon became obsessed about going home and talked about it continually. Though she enjoyed all her visits, brief or extended, the vacations were always her favorite. The trouble was that every time she came for an extended period, she believed she was going to stay at home for good. When Mother packed up her things to take her back to Pennhurst after her longer visits, Bev would wail and cry, "I don't want to go back to Pennhurst!" Who could blame her? Mother's heart ached to hear it as they put her in the car to take her away from her beloved home and drive her back to a place she hated. When I was a child, I couldn't understand why they had to do it. Of course, during this early period Mother still considered Pennhurst a boarding school, a temporary placement, where Bev would learn and grow and develop according to her limited abilities. She truly believed that one day Bev wouldn't have to go back there and that her wish to go home, and stay home, could come true.

The big change in her relationship with her family came in June 1957, when Bev reached her fourteenth birthday. Correspondence with Pennhurst shows that when Mother asked for permission to take Bev home for her accustomed birthday vacation, she was told that it was not advisable at that time. By now, Bev was well into her adolescence and undergoing the changes that any teenager would be experiencing, both physical and emotional. These changes certainly affected her behavior and made managing it much more difficult for both the Pennhurst staff and our parents. She continued to become more abusive both to herself and others. When she was agitated she bit herself, scratched herself, banged her head against the wall, and lashed out at others, staff and fellow residents alike. Her violent behavior began to isolate her from everyone, including her own family. The sad truth is that our affection for our sister was slowly but surely eroded away by her erratic and aggressive behavior. At times I myself actually came to fear her, especially as she grew older and stronger. Our parents went to Pennhurst to talk to the presiding doctor about these developments and agreed that having Bev at home would not be a good idea. I'm sure our parents were becoming concerned about being able to control her at home and felt safer visiting her at Pennhurst instead. As a result, until new medications and improved behavior modification programs were implemented, her interaction with the family became less frequent and more strained. Sadly, after their consultation with the doctor at Pennhurst in July of 1957, Bev never came home for a vacation again. Though she still came home occasionally for day visits, her vacations were over. Unfortunately, once Bev stopped coming home for vacations, it was easy for the rest of us to lose touch with her. Although we continued to visit her at Pennhurst, the fact that she so rarely came home anymore widened the gap between us.

Coming home was the most important thing in Bev's life. When she was home, she craved the attention of her parents, who were her undying source of affection and the absolute center of her world. Though she needed them desperately, she did not really need us. Quite frankly, Bev was not particularly interested in her siblings. She got us mixed up, our names interchangeable, and she continued to grow increasingly detached from us. As we were growing up and changing into people she didn't recognize, she didn't really know us anymore. That was true for us as well, as her physical appearance began to change drastically. She was developing into a young woman instead of a little girl and, because we saw her so infrequently, her new body came as a shock to us. Not only was she beginning to look like an adult, she was also gaining weight, on her way to becoming obese. With her buzz haircut, bad teeth, and a body covered with bruises and bite marks, she no longer resembled the sister we knew. We couldn't comprehend what was happening to her, and no one explained it to us. In those days there was no family counseling available to help us cope. Our parents did the best they could, but in the end we children were left to deal with circumstances we didn't understand. In our confusion, we backed away and stopped trying to relate to Bev, until she was a sister in name only.

By 1957 I had turned ten years old and Jonnie seven, old enough to accompany our parents when they visited Bev at Pennhurst. This is when Jonnie and I became more intimately acquainted with the institution. Our brother Greg, who was by then fifteen years old, already had a part time job that took up much of his free time. With working and school activities and hanging out with his friends, he really had no time to go along with us. Besides, as a teenager, Greg tended to be very independent and didn't participate in a lot of family activities, including visiting Bev. Jonnie and I, on the other hand, spent many a Sunday afternoon at Pennhurst.

In the beginning Jonnie and I didn't go onto the hospital grounds with my parents. Instead we waited outside the main gate while they went onto the campus. According to our parents there were regulations about young children entering the hospital complex. There was a small guard shack near the gate with someone inside who could keep an eye on us while we waited. The surrounding area was pleasant with grass and trees, a big water tower, and a sprawling vista of brick buildings not far beyond. To us it was like a park, and we enjoyed playing together as we waited. For us it was a fun afternoon, with an entertaining ride through the countryside and free time to play. When we were older, and began to accompany our parents inside, it was a different story.

Once our car passed through the gates and onto the hospital grounds, we left the lovely countryside behind and entered a maze of imposing brick buildings. Many of these buildings had rows of rectangular win-

dows that were covered with metal protective gratings. Behind those gratings were the unfortunate souls imprisoned in locked buildings where they spent their long, dreary days. Through those windows we could hear the screams. Persistent wailing, howling, and screeching filled the air. To my sister and me these cries weren't mournful or plaintive, they were terrifying. We couldn't imagine what kind of creatures could be making these sounds. They sounded like wild animals. We didn't know that there were just ordinary human beings in there.

Our parents rarely took us inside the buildings in those days, whether by their choice or because of some particular regulations, I don't know. That was fine with us. We didn't want to go inside the place where the noises came from. Besides the noise, there was also the smell. Wafting out the open windows, in the days before air conditioning, was a permeating odor of disinfectant that made the whole place smell like a recently scoured toilet. It was like an invisible fog that swirled around us. When Bev came out the door, the odor clung to her like an alien perfume. The last thing we wanted to do was go inside where the smell and the noises came from. We were happy to stay outside and watch the parade of visitors and residents come and go.

While one of our parents went inside to get Bev, the other waited outside with us. Most of the time my little sister and I stayed in the car and stared out the window. The residents who were free to walk about looked strange to us. Some of them tapped on the windows of the car and peered in at us. Some shuffled by like zombies, staring straight ahead, barely aware of their surroundings. Some were grossly disfigured. Some were physically disabled, palsied or crippled, and moved erratically. Most were dressed in clothes that didn't fit and were often mismatched. It was a pathetic parade of forlorn souls, although they were the lucky ones - at least they were outdoors.

If we ventured outside the car, many of the residents came up to us. They tried to talk to us, often in slurred speech or unintelligible language. Very often they wanted to touch us or hold our hands. Jonnie and I were appalled at their overtures. When we saw someone approach us, we ran away or hid behind our father. Dad, however, did not try to avoid them. He talked to them and joked with them and made nonsensical conversation. He tried to make it seem oddly normal. His interactions with them disturbed me as I watched him cross an invisible line into their strange world, leaving my sister and me behind.

Mother, on the other hand, did not interact with any of the residents. As we sat in the car she pressed her lips together and stared past them. When it was time to get out of the car she ignored them. She wanted no part of their bizarre world. When she was with Bev she focused entirely upon her and tried to provide her with a safe little bubble that kept those other people and their chaotic world away from her, if only for a few precious minutes. While Dad seemed to be trying to make the best of a difficult situation, Mother tried to rise above it and will it away. Both of our parents were dealing with pain and frustration and guilt, but chose different ways of coping with it. During our visits there was a constant tension between their two opposite approaches to the situation. Jonnie and I, as usual, were caught in the middle. Our visitations were fraught with angst. Not only did we have to deal with the disturbing physical surroundings of the institution and the upsetting appearance and behavior of our older sister, but we had to endure the tension and constant friction between our parents in already stressful circumstances.

Once Bev came out to the car, the visits usually progressed the same way. When the weather was nice we searched out one of the picnic tables on the grounds where we could all sit down together. Here we gave Bev candy and other treats, a cake and gifts if it was her birthday. Bev loved to eat. Eating was the only thing that seemed to make her happy and the one thing that was sure to calm her down. The reason that Bev continued to gain weight year after year was that everyone used food as a tranquilizer. When all else failed, we gave her candy. Licorice was her favorite and even the promise of licorice was enough to quell a tantrum. Though food was the main attraction, we tried to entertain Bev as best we could by singing or reciting nursery rhymes or repeating the nonsense she chanted. Our parents tried to engage her in conversation, but Bev found that tiresome. My mother fussed over the latest scratches or bruises, her short cropped hair, her disheveled appearance. My father teased her and tickled her.

The other residents out and about on the grounds pestered us relentlessly. They craved attention and peppered our parents with endless questions. They wanted to hold our hands and hug us. Of course they were attracted by the food we spread out on the tables. We learned that it was best not to give them any treats. If we did, they often became aggressive and gave us no peace at all. Once they realized we weren't going to share the goodies, they usually wandered away disappointed, hoping to find a new source of attention. Many of them never had any visitors to give them affection or bring them gifts or candy. Some of them needed more attention than anyone could ever give and sought it ceaselessly like sharks cruising through the ocean. If the weather was not good, we often sat in the car and conducted our visit there rather than using the depressing indoor visiting area. Sometimes, however, we just had to remain inside, where the lack of privacy was even more of an issue in the crowded buildings. Though our parents chose to remain outside whenever possible, when our brother and his family began going to see Bev on their own, they more often visited indoors.

Greg's two daughters told me stories about some of the visits they made there with their parents in the early 1970's. Their older daughter Lesley remembers one occasion when a tall, lanky girl came over to their family to ask for some food. She reached for a bottle of Coke, but instead of taking a drink from it, she banged it on the edge of the table and shattered it. Howling wildly, she scooped up the shards of green glass and began scoring her arms and wrists with them. Several attendants quickly responded by wrapping her in a straight jacket and hauling the shrieking young woman away as the children watched in horror. On another occasion the staff had offered the use of one of the offices for Bev's family visit in order to provided some privacy and to prevent such incidents. Unfortunately, even that attempt didn't provide security. One of Bev's friends, who was unhappy to be excluded from the festivities, stood screaming outside the office door. When no one offered to let her in, she punched her fist through the glazed window glass in the door and made a bloody mess before being restrained by the attendants. Why they had glass windows in these doors I don't understand. This wasn't an isolated incident. Months later, during one of her tantrums, Bev also put her hand through a window and suffered nasty lacerations. When these old buildings were constructed, safety simply wasn't a major concern, and lack of funds in later years made it impossible to correct all the potential hazards.

Greg's girls both remember being traumatized by these events and by the sights and sounds inside those dreadful buildings. They tell about seeing padded walls and wondering why anyone would put gymnastic mats on a wall. They remember the horrible smell and compared it to the underground public bathroom in Reading's center square. They cringed at the ever present sounds of moaning and screaming echoing through the hallways, and they hid behind their parents to avoid the unwanted physical contact with the odd looking occupants who wanted to squeeze and pinch the cute little girls. Despite these terrors, they preferred to stay inside with their parents rather than remain outside alone in the car. Just as Jonnie and I remember the patients peering in the windows and pounding on the glass, they also remember the same behavior. Even worse, they recount a time when a group of curious residents actually started rocking the car back and forth, while the two of them huddled on the floor in terror. Until they told me these stories, I hadn't realized that they had experienced the same traumatizing events that Jonnie and I had when we were youngsters. Sadly, the haunting legacy of Pennhurst had passed from one generation to the next.

Whether inside or out, the visits at Pennhurst didn't last long. Once the food was eaten and gifts opened, Bev became restless. Besides singing some songs and taking a short walk, there was not much else to do. Conversation really didn't mean much to Bev. She would answer "yes or no" questions or repeat what was said to her. She obsessed about food, pleaded about going home, and whined about other residents hitting her. She wasn't interested in games or puppets or coloring. She preferred to rock back and forth and play with her fingers, which seemed to suggest what she probably spent most of her day doing. In about an hour or so, we were all ready to leave. After whining for awhile, Bev trudged resolutely back to one of the brick buildings with her mother or father. A few minutes later, the rest of us piled back into the car for the depressing ride home.

Though I didn't listen carefully, I caught parts of the conversations between my parents on those drives home. These were not pleasant conversations. My mother was often upset by Bev's appearance. For many years Bev sported bruises and bite marks all over her body, many of them self inflicted. For quite a few years Bev pulled out her hair, banged her head against the wall, and bit herself on the arms and hands. But some of the bruises could not have been her doing. Any mother would be angry at the thought of anyone hurting her child. Was she being accosted by other residents? Was she being restrained too roughly by staff? My mother asked many questions. She got very few answers.

Mother was also upset by the fact that Bev's possessions routinely disappeared. She bought her clothing and toys and personal items, carefully labeling each with an indelible pen as instructed. Our relatives also often sent her gifts. Nevertheless, when Bev came home, or we visited her at Pennhurst, more often than not she was wearing someone else's clothes, most of which fit poorly, while she had none of the toiletries or personal things my mother had so lovingly picked out for her. Everything was destroyed or stolen or mislaid, either by residents or staff, who could say? There simply were not enough staff to give residents individual attention let alone take care of their possessions. This lack of personal possessions was just one more way in which Bev was swallowed up by the institution. Just as her possessions disappeared, so did pieces of her personality, until she was unrecognizable to us anymore. Beverley Lynne Miller had become a changeling, the true Bev lost to us forever.

Although the visits we made to Pennhurst together were supposed to be a chance for Jonnie and me to have some close contact with our older sister, our interaction with her during them was minimal. For the most part we just stood back and watched the scene unfold like a tragic play. There was little affectionate connection between us and Bev. From our point of view, she belonged to that community of strange folk who roamed the grounds and halls of Pennhurst. As far as she was concerned, the visits were all about her parents. She wanted them to herself and we just got in the way. She didn't really want us there, so, after awhile, we didn't want to be there either. It's no wonder that when we grew to be teenagers and our parents said, "We're going to visit Bev on Sunday. Do you want to come along?" our answer was usually "no." We went sometimes out of guilt or duty, not because we wanted to.

Actually, once we were old enough to stay at home alone, visiting Bev was voluntary for us, not required or even encouraged. Even though the visits were certainly not fun, we did occasionally go along because Bev was our sister and we felt we should see her. As we got older we realized that, but for a twist of fate, it could have been either of us who had been the unlucky one who got locked away. What I don't understand is that, though we did sometimes visit her, we didn't do anything more. We never made or bought her gifts to take along when we visited. We never even took her what our mother would call a "doofalolly" - some small token like a souvenir from a trip or a silly toy or a poster of the latest rock and roll idol. Back home we weren't encouraged to write to her or send her cards. Though Mother insisted that we send birthday cards to other relatives, she rarely suggested that we send one to Bev. Though these are the things we would do for other family members, we didn't routinely do them for our sister.

Whether by accident or design, our parents seemed almost purposefully to erase Bev from our lives. I have never seen a photograph of our early visits with Bev at Pennhurst. Though Jonnie and I had gone along with our parents to visit Bev for years, we have only our memories of the time we spent there, no visual record. Not only are there no pictures of her at Pennhurst, for a long period of time there are no pictures of her at all. Although before she went away there are many pictures of Bev in our family album, except for a few photos taken in Sinking Spring in 1957, we have no photographs of her either at Pennhurst or at home. Even though Greg and Jonnie and I continue to appear in the album, our parents had stopped taking pictures of Bev.

Pennhurst State Hospital was a forbidding Wonderland, a foreign landscape filled with outlandish characters who existed in a parallel universe but who were invisible to the outside world. Once Bev plunged down the rabbit hole into that land, she too became invisible, fading from sight until she vanished from our lives altogether and existed only there, in that place where we were the strangers. It seemed to work both ways, as she lost sight of us, as well, the longer she was there. She had only her memories to cling to as she fell further and further away from us and was swept up in the madness.

~9~

The Great Divide

The final blow to Bev's dreams of home was our parents' divorce in November 1965. The split destroyed our home and fractured our family forever. Though our parents loved each other very much, their reasons for getting married couldn't have been more different. One day when I was nine or ten years old, Mother and I were chatting in the kitchen as she was preparing our dinner. "Why do people get married?" I asked. "To have children," she answered without hesitation. She firmly believed that and dedicated her life to that end. For her, marriage was all about having children and creating a safe and happy home for them. I never asked my father that question, but I knew the answer. He was looking for a mother, not for future children, but for himself. For him, a wife provided the mother he never had growing up. As a result, he spent his whole marriage competing with his own children for his wife's attention. While Mother was committed to her marriage and family, Dad was committed to being a child himself. When I was a young folksinger I learned the Leonard Cohen song "Bird on a Wire." I have never heard a more perfect description of my dad. He tried in his way to be free, and hurt everyone he loved in the process.

To say that Dad avoided commitment is an understatement. During his lifetime he jumped from job to job, house to house, and woman to woman. He was a salesman, and a good one, who could talk anyone into anything. He kept questing for the perfect job that would make his fortune and had dozens of jobs. He sold cars, photo albums, stone facings for houses, home appliances, encyclopedias, insurance, and soap. When he sold milk, we had all the milk we could drink, when he sold soda, we had all the soda we could drink, when he sold beer and whiskey, he had all the alcohol he could drink. He was a lifelong alcoholic and working for the beer and whiskey companies gave him a legitimate excuse for hanging out in barrooms, where he could talk for hours and buy drinks for all his "good friends." He made many of his sales calls in the evenings, which gave him a legitimate excuse to visit the houses of many a lonely lady who had more interest in Dad than in whatever he was selling. He preferred jobs where he could work on commission and make his own schedule, so that he had lots of time for his extracurricular activities. While our mother sat in front of a microscope on an assembly line day after tedious day, he spent most of his time in barrooms and bedrooms and handball courts.

His drinking and philandering played havoc with his marriage and placed our mother in the role of a long suffering martyr. For years she struggled to keep the family fed and clothed while Dad spent all his money, and hers too. After a series of jobs as waitress, store clerk, and telemarketer, she landed a coveted production line position at Western Electric and brought in regular paychecks, while he skipped from job to job and had many months of "layoffs". When times were good, they were good, and when they were bad, they were very bad. There were times when Dad was reduced to pilfering our lunch money to buy gas for his car. Half of our phone calls were from bill collectors. We were instructed to answer the phone when it rang so that we could put creditors off by telling them our parents were out. If the doorbell rang unexpectedly, we dutifully went to the door to lie about our parents' whereabouts. It was not the script for a happy home life.

The downward slide towards divorce began in January of 1961 when we moved to Wyomissing, a suburb of Reading. This move represented a major transition for all of us. Our parents were finally becoming financially more stable and, even though creditors continued to hound us, most of the bills somehow got paid. Wyomissing was an upscale community that included many of the area's most prestigious families and boasted many grand houses. The far northern border of this borough was Penn Avenue, the main thoroughfare running from center city, through West Reading, and on to the furthest reaches of the bus line in Sinking Spring. Although it was primarily a business route, there were also quite a few modest homes clustered along the way, mixed in with the stores, doctors' and lawyers' offices, small businesses, and a community firehouse. Our family rented half a brick twin, literally just on the right side of the tracks. Across the street from us was a railroad track that paralleled the avenue. When trains went by, the whole house shook and the noise was so loud that all conversation stopped until the last car had passed. It was like some sort of vaudeville comedy routine. A group of people are gathered in the living room chatting away, a train comes by, everyone freezes in position, then resumes the conversation, never missing a beat, as the last car passes through. After awhile we didn't even notice anymore.

Penn Avenue branched off just before our house. The business route continued heading west while our branch, a quieter residential street opposite the train tracks, ended after only a few blocks. Our house, situated on the corner of an alley and the main street, was a brick twin with a small patch of grass out front and cement steps leading up to a large covered porch. In the rear of the house was a small fenced yard with a gnarled crab apple tree in the center, a garden border, and a cement walk. A gravel alley ran alongside the yard, then turned into a paved alley that ran behind all the houses on the block and led to detached garages. Our landlord, an old World War I veteran with a thick Pennsylvania Dutch accent, lived right next door. His watery blue eyes were buried in deep wrinkles, permanently stained with coal dust, that made him look positively ancient. He was a penny pinching old bachelor, fussy and set in his ways, but he seemed to like having children around and offered us candy when we went to his door once a month with the rent check. He was a lonely old soul who loved to talk, and when he had a captive audience it was hard to get away. He was one of the only people I ever met who could out talk our father.

Typical of twins, the house was narrow and deep. The first room downstairs was a living room, then a dining room, then the kitchen in the back, with a door leading out to the yard. Next to the door was a toilet, not a powder room, just a toilet. Upstairs were three bedrooms and a bath. Our parents had the front bedroom, Greg the middle, and Jonnie and I the rear. Though it was a plain and simple home, to us it was the height of luxury after the old farmhouse in Sinking Spring. It had central heating that kept us toasty warm in every room, it had storm windows and screens, it had doors on the bedrooms and bathroom, it had closets and kitchen cabinets. Our parents bought new furniture and rugs, and decorated the living room with pictures and pillows and knick knacks. It looked like a real home. Compared to the fancy houses and mansions just a few blocks away it was humble indeed. But this house, humble as it was, placed us on the edge of a new level of society.

With both of our parents working, our financial situation improved considerably and our father began to have dreams of moving up in the world. I think some of this ambition was fostered by the relationships he had at the health clubs that he joined to play handball and racquetball. He was a very good player, and the lawyers and doctors and businessmen that belonged to the club enjoyed competing with him. He was also a skilled tennis player and began playing tennis matches with the social elite. His friendships with these men made him want to belong to their social circles as well. By moving to Wyomissing, an upscale community, he felt he could enter their world. Our parents began frequenting social clubs and attending parties where they would hob nob with the local rich and famous. Not surprisingly, their efforts were in vain, and the Millers remained on the bottom rungs of the social ladder.

The move to Wyomissing turned our lives upside down. Almost immediately, everyone was unhappy. Although our future appeared promising, what our father was hoping would be a renaissance for our family became a disaster. I'm sure that our parents were more pleased than we were to leave the drafty old house at the end of the bus line for a cozy, newer house much closer to town. For Jonnie and me, even though we loved our new bedroom with the butterfly wallpaper, the bathroom with a real door, the modern kitchen, and the warmth of central heating, the move was upsetting. We missed our old house, old neighborhood, old schools and, most of all, our old friends. Our parents' thrill at the idea of moving up in society was lost on us. We found out soon enough that we didn't fit in and could never really be part of the life lived by the rich kids. We spent the rest of our school years as outsiders, living on the fringes of a world that did not welcome newcomers without the proper credentials.

Our parents soon realized that they would never have enough money to keep up with the Joneses. The doors to the inner circle remained firmly shut to the likes of us. It literally drove my father to drink. He always had been a drinker, but he now became a true alcoholic. Our parents began to drink together at home, which they had never done before. Dad began staying out late every night, supposedly working. By the time he came home, Mother had long since gone to bed alone. She knew very well where he was, and we soon began to understand as well. The situation went from bad to worse when he traded in his frequent dalliances for a steady girlfriend. That was the final straw. Our mother, who had always tolerated our father's bad behavior like an angel, began spreading her wings with newfound confidence. Unfortunately for Dad, a lot of that confidence came from the man who had begun driving her to and from work when we moved to Wyomissing. It was not long before he became much more than just the fellow that provided transportation. He began to provide a lot more.

Another change that had a profound effect on all of us, parents and children alike, was attending a new church. Within a year or so after our move, Dad became disenchanted with our old church, a feeling that I believe was mutual, and decided that we should leave and join the Lutheran church in Wyomissing. It was a stately stone building, beautifully renovated with plush carpeting and softly padded pews. The pastor was a charming, handsome intellectual who headed a well heeled congregation that included quite a few of the local pillars of society. It couldn't have been more different from the one we had left. It was a lovely church, but it didn't work for us and, before very long, we stopped going to church as a family. All the support that our family had had during our years in our old church was gone. That church, with its strong pastor and strict Lutheran doctrine, had been the glue that helped hold our family together. Without it the marriage soon fell apart, then the family fell apart, and gradually our whole world fell apart. We began to drift, each in a different direction. All of us became lost, including Bev.

Indeed, dark days were ahead for Bev. By the time we moved to Wyomissing she was a young adult of eighteen, and her relationship with the family continued to deteriorate. Greg was away attending college and got married as soon as he graduated, Jonnie and I were alienated teenagers, and our parents were drifting apart into eventual divorce. It was not a warm and fuzzy family time. Bev herself was no longer a child, but rather a young woman who, had she not been mentally handicapped, would have been off to college or holding down a job or getting married. Being away from home was, by that time, almost a natural separation. She no longer came to our house for visits, and our vists to Pennhurst to see her became more and more infrequent. What little time we spent with Bev was not pleasant. These were difficult years for her in Pennhurst. She had no hair, she had no teeth, she was overweight, she was battered and bruised, most often from self abuse, but also from altercations with other residents. As Bev's behavior continued to deteriorate, she was more difficult to manage and less responsive to social interaction with anyone, including our family. She was unhappy, she rarely smiled, she was over medicated. As her condition worsened, visits became less frequent and, as visits became less frequent, her condition worsened. We were all caught in a classic Catch-22

When the split finally became a reality, we three siblings were already separated by circumstance. Greg had left our house when he married in May of 1964, and he and his wife Chris were living with their infant daughter in a little town just south of Reading. He was working as an elementary school art teacher and attending graduate night classes at Temple University. His hands were full as he built a life for himself and his new family. Prior to the divorce, Mother confided in him and depended on him for both moral and practical support. Afterwards, as much as he may have wanted to help out, he didn't have a lot of time to deal with what was happening with Jonnie and me.

I, myself, had just started my freshman year at college. I was very immature and having a difficult time adjusting to college life. Because I didn't drive, I lived on campus even though the school was only half an hour away from home. I was struggling and needed the safety net of a family that no longer existed. Jonnie was a high school sophomore, a vulnerable teenager, trying to cope with very little guidance. Since I had left for college in September, leaving her on her own, she bore the brunt of the divorce on the home front. Loneliness was a huge problem for her as she rattled around an empty house on her own. Circumstances had conspired to pull the three of us siblings apart and made it difficult for us to help each other through these tough times. The rug had been pulled out from under us and sent us all flying.

Though we had known for some time that our parents were not getting along, and that each of them had a new romantic interest, the divorce itself came as a surprise to me when it finally happened. I came home from college for Thanksgiving vacation to find that my parents had parted ways and that my father had been banished from the house. In keeping with our unhealthy family dynamic, we had never sat down together to talk about trouble in the marriage or the possibility of a breakup. There was no preparation, physically or psychologically, for dealing with the drastic changes we would face after a divorce. There was no gradual move from one situation to the next. It was sudden and catastrophic. Indeed, our dad was blindsided by the actual deed. He was served with divorce papers and the door was locked. Period. I came home from college for Thanksgiving vacation to find that my dad had been kicked out of the house and was not allowed back in under any circumstances. Unfortunately, our mother didn't know any other way to handle the situation. In her life she had so little experience in standing up for herself that, when she finally decided to do it, she was almost ruthless in her determination.

Divorce was not as common in those days as it is now, and there was a greater stigma attached to it. Most couples just stuck it out for the sake of the kids, which is what our mother did for a long time. Though she probably would have preferred to wait until Jonnie had graduated from high school, when the opportunity to get out of the marriage presented itself, she seized it. The actual divorce proceedings were engineered by her boyfriend, who had already gone through the procedure himself when he divorced his wife and won custody of his two young sons. Under his tutelage she went through the process, keeping the developments secret from everyone. As the eldest, Greg had the best idea of what was going on. Mother had actually discussed the situation with him and had given him some warning of the impending legal action. Since Jonnie still lived full time at home, she witnessed the events leading up to the split first hand. As for myself, I knew the marriage was in trouble, but I was naively unaware of the possibility of divorce until it was a done deal.

Our mother became a different person once her husband was out of her life. She spent a lot of time going out with her boyfriend, and, worse as far as we were concerned, she brought her boyfriend into our home. When I came home from school on weekends, I often found Jonnie in tears. Unfortunately, during that first year of the divorce I was not emotionally able to be much help to her. Being away from home for the first time and being forced to grow up fast overwhelmed me. I became nervous, worried and melancholy, and my usually excellent grades plummeted. When I got home I found a cold, empty house and a sad and deserted younger sister. With Mother out with her boyfriend much of the time, Jonnie and I were on our own. We trudged up to the local market to buy a few provisions and scraped together some meager meals. Feeling completely abandoned, we sat around the empty house wondering just what was going on.

At first I was totally naive about our mother's new romantic relationship. One evening Mother took the bus into town, telling us she was going to meet a friend. As the night wore on and I realized that the last bus had come and gone and Mother was still not home, I became very worried. As it got later and later, I panicked and called my brother to ask him what I should do. He knew that Mother was out on a date and told me not to worry, even though he didn't explain that to me. Much later, when she finally came home smiling and happy, I was angry. The truth finally hit me, and I became resentful. I felt like a fool for worrying about her all night while she had been out having a wonderful time. She was the one acting like a teenager, forcing me to take on the role of the responsible parent. I was not happy with the new arrangement.

Jonnie and I commiserated with each other and kept each other company, but we felt lost and betrayed. Soon, however, we discovered a way to make ourselves feel better. All of our negative feelings found an outlet in rebellion. We had one unshakable common bond - we hated our mother's boyfriend. We focused all our pain and frustration on him. We treated him as badly as we possibly could, with all of the adolescent vengeance we could muster. And, typical of our mother's approach, she did not sit down and discuss our feelings with us. Instead, she tried to force us to accept him, driving the wedge ever deeper.

Mother dreamed of making us one big happy family and set out to make her dream come true much too soon. Not long after we had spent our first Thanksgiving without our dad, she took us out with her boyfriend to select a Christmas tree. Jonnie and I followed them around the tree lot sullenly as they chose the perfect specimen. Actually, this was the first time Mother had ever gotten to pick out her own tree. Dad always waited until Christmas Eve to shop for a tree, when the cost would be half price. More than once he came home with a motley little pine because he had waited too long and the lots were closing down. He came racing in at the last minute, cursing as he tried to set up the tree before we went to church. Jesus' name was invoked many times, though not in the spirit of the season. This time Mother would have her tree in plenty of time to decorate and place packages before Christmas Eve arrived. Unfortunately, Jonnie and I did not share her enthusiasm. For us, our first Christmas without Dad was a dreary event, and we went through the motions like a pair of zombies.

Once the divorce was a done deed, the full measure of Mother's anger and resentment washed over us all like a tidal wave. The effect upon all of us was profound. All of our hearts were broken, all of our lives changed radically, and all of us reaped a bitter harvest in the years to come. I believe her own hostility toward our father blinded her to the fact that we still loved him. Children do. No matter what he was guilty of, he was still our father and we missed him terribly. Even though she was able to cut him out of her life, she should not have expected us to do the same. She sincerely believed that we were as glad to be rid of him as she was. She couldn't see how wrong she was. Instead, we extended our rebellion even further. Not only did we totally reject the boyfriend, we continued to see our father and joined in a perverse alliance with him. We were rebels with a common enemy.

In the early days following the divorce, our father made it easy for us to see him. He rented an apartment a few blocks away, easy walking distance for us. His purpose was to remain as close to his home as possible, not only to stay in contact with us, but to spy on his ex-wife and her beau. He was truly devastated by the divorce, never expecting to be exiled from his own home. Before our mother met her new man, she would never have dreamed of taking matters into her own hands. Her lover had provoked it all, and our father knew it. During his entire marriage he had always depended on the fact that his wife believed that marriage was a permanent arrangement and that raising her family was paramount. She had always been forgiving and long suffering. The girlfriends, the drinking, the spending of every hard earned penny were all tolerated by a good Christian woman with low self esteem. Enter the white knight in a black Pontiac. Our father had finally met his match.

After the divorce, Jonnie and I developed an unhealthy relationship with our father. We visited him in his apartment, sat drinking cheap wine and sulking like conspirators in a Shakespearean drama. We spied for him and reported back on what was happening in our house. He used us to get information about our mother's new life, he used us to vent his own anger and self pity, and he used us to borrow money when we had a few extra dollars to spare. As soon as he could arrange it, he rented a house even closer to our house than the apartment had been and set up an insurance office. It must have made our mother furious. It gave the three of us perverse satisfaction.

Before long our mother's anger with our father began to isolate her from her children. Once our father was out of the picture, she was free to spend as much time as she wanted with her new romantic interest, a younger man who had taken her under his protective wing. It's understandable that she wanted to be happy and spend time with someone who found her desirable and worthy of respect. Even though we thought he was a complete dork, with his crewcut hair and white socks, Mother obviously adored him. This was something that Jonnie and I could deal with, but we couldn't tolerate her attempts at forcing us to reject our father and accept a replacement. That was a huge mistake on her part. She just wasn't strong enough to make it on her own. She needed her mentor in every way and was unable to make a move without him. Because of that total dependence, she desperately wanted us to approve of him and make a place for him in our lives. She never expected to meet the kind of resistance that we put up, and I'm sure she blamed our father for encouraging our rebellion. As a result, she became angry with us. She turned that anger on us by shutting us out of her life for a period of time. We barely spoke. The atmosphere in the house was arctic. She had drawn the battle lines, but Jonnie and I were defiant teenagers. This was a battle she could not win.

As a result, Jonnie and I found ourselves in a difficult position. We were two unhappy teenagers dealing with two unhappy parents who were acting like teenagers. Our brother Greg, nearly overwhelmed with his responsibilities to his own family as well as his job and graduate school, distanced himself from the house in Wyomissing and all the conflicts in and around it. Just as I was puzzled by the lack of support from extended family or church in our lives when it came to dealing with problems surrounding Bev, I have to say that we had the same lack of support surrounding the divorce. Jonnie and I received no phone calls or visits, no advice or sympathy, no obvious concern for our welfare from anyone. Because we were teenagers, not youngsters, I believe everyone, including our mother and brother, expected us to be able to weather the divorce on our own.

This total lack of support caused us to become both independent and rebellious. Because of our individual personalities, position in the family, and past experiences, we found different ways of responding. At first we both fell apart. Then we needed to find a way to go on, and we took very different paths. My sister sought out new friends, including boyfriends, experimented with drugs, and became, in many ways, self destructive. I, on the other hand, became overly self protective. I withdrew into myself and became distrustful of everyone except my best friend Charlotte, who was my ever faithful ally. After my initial meltdown, I formed a hard exterior and hid behind a barrier of disdain and feigned sophistication. No one realized how dreadfully unhappy both Jonnie and I were. We seemed to be handling everything just fine. Indeed, I'm sure to others we seemed very selfish and self serving, as we gave our mother a hard time. The truth is that we weren't handling it well at all, and the cavalry did not appear on the horizon to rescue us.

Greg, Jonnie, and I wound up having to deal with the fallout of the divorce for our entire adult lives. The divorce was bitter on my mother's side and martyred on my father's side. Our mother felt that the divorce was payback for all the indignities she had suffered with her husband through the years. She felt liberated and avenged by tossing our father out with nothing but his personal possessions. Our father, on the other hand, felt cheated and victimized. He thought that our mother's actions were unnecessarily harsh and punitive. He appointed her lover the villain in the scenario. He was sure that if that man were ever to step out of the picture that he could step back in and make amends. Until the day Mother died, Dad held out hope that one day the two of them would get back together and live in blissful reconciliation.

The divorce changed everything. It pulled us apart and flung us all in different directions, both literally and figuratively. In the years right after the divorce, our mother centered her life around her lover while our father broke up with his steady girlfriend and found companionship with a series of new women. Greg devoted himself to his family, his job, and his church. Jonnie finished high school and moved to Philadelphia to find work and attend art school. I graduated from college, quickly found a position at a public library near my boyfriend's home, and got my own apartment. We all suffered, we all struggled, but we all survived and, after many years, we came together as a family redefined. But, in the meantime, there was chaos, and in the midst of it Bev was all but forgotten. She, in her innocence and isolation, was the most unfortunate victim of the whole mess.

During the time that our family was in the throes of dealing with the divorce back home, Bev was experiencing her own major life change at Pennhurst. In her case, the change was all for the good as Pennhurst began to comply with policies mandated by newly passed mental health legislation in the 1960's. Unfortunately, while all these developments were taking place to make Bev's Pennhurst existence better, her family was falling apart, and Bev's emotional needs were being neglected. Just when Bev needed her family to complement the improvements in her life at Pennhurst, we were not there for her. By 1965, the year of her parents' divorce, Bev was 22 years old. She was an adult. Now she had to make her own way in the world just like the rest of us, and for the next twenty years her world would still be Pennhurst.

Bev was living in a C cottage in 1966 when the Pennsylvania Health and Mental Retardation Act was passed and Pennhurst started to implement changes that were needed to comply with the new law. In October of 1966, just a year after their divorce, our parents received a form letter explaining what was happening in Bev's unit. The letter states that a new program was being put in place to improve living conditions in the unit, and that extra workers were being assigned there to allow more individual attention for each girl. Special emphasis was to be placed on establishing self care habits and teaching the girls skills they needed for daily living. Along with these improvements came the idea for a PTA, a Parent-Trainers Association. Parents were invited to attend a meeting with the staff to discuss the new program and the formation of the PTA.

Meetings of the newly formed PTA continued to be held monthly at Pennhurst to make plans for activities for the girls. For instance, during the summer of 1967 some of the families of girls in Bev's cottage organized picnics that were held on the Pennhurst grounds and were very popular. Since not all families participated, each family that did come took another girl into their care for the picnic and provided food for her. Form letters sent to our parents that year reported on the positive outcomes of the program. As the staff saw improvement in the girls' behavior and toilet habits, some of them were able to leave their cottages to take regular meals in the dining hall. Eventually, some of them were even able to go out into the community. Permission slips were given to parents to fill out so that girls could go on day trips off the Pennhurst campus. Finally they were learning to live like "normal" young women.

During this time more attention also was paid to health care for the patients, and late in 1966, after being hospitalized with a fever, Bev was given a thorough physical exam. By this time she was very obese, weighing 216 pounds at just 5 feet 4. Otherwise she was in fairly good shape except for her teeth, which were badly decayed. For many years Bev had been plagued with dental problems. Since it was difficult to work on her in the dental chair, her visits to the dentist at Pennhurst were few and not always successful. They were obviously unpleasant experiences for Bev who, to this day, still talks about having a toothache and going to the dentist. Because of this neglect, her teeth simply began to rot away. In January of 1967 she finally had dental surgery under general anesthesia to remove all of her teeth once and for all. As a result Bev has been toothless since the age of twenty four. Because of her limited mental capacity, she was unable to wear dentures successfully. Though this never inhibited her ability to eat, one of her favorite activities, it did alter her appearance, giving her a premature sagging of the cheeks and a granny-like toothless grin.

One of the new policies at Pennhurst was to encourage families to interact more with their relatives who were residing there. Parents were prompted to send cards and letters to their children and to visit as often as possible. Staff took photos of residents at events such as holiday parties and sent them home to their families, along with personal notes. More formal communications from social workers explained behavior modification models, educational experiences, and community interaction. Progress reports were sent on a regular basis. At the time, however, these letters were being delivered to our newly divorced parents who were not inclined to work cooperatively for Bev's welfare, whether to attend meetings or activities, or even visit their daughter.

Between August 1967, while all the promising changes at Pennhurst were taking place, and July 1968 there is no correspondence in Bev's patient file. However, in August 1968 a very significant letter shows up. It is very obvious by this letter's content that Bev was being sadly neglected by her parents. This heartbreaking letter states:

Your daughter Beverly has been very disturbed lately because she has not had visitors in such a long time. We feel that you would notice a change in Beverly if you would come to Pennhurst. She is no longer abusive and is now responsive to people. The ward personnel report that she talks about her family often and cries because she has not seen any of you.

The letter says that Bev was upset about not having visitors "in such a long time". It isn't clear just what a "long time" could have been, but a visitation record slipped in among her files is very revealing. This record is in the form of a printed card from Bev's cottage on which visitors were obliged to sign their names. This card tells a revealing story. It lists only nine visits between June 1963 and April 1970. If this is a true record of the actual visits Bev had during these seven years, it is no wonder that she was upset. In 1963 there were three visits, the dates reflecting the usual ones that we made most years - one for her birthday in June, one for Thanksgiving and one for Christmas. These entries were signed by Mother and show that both parents, as well as Jonnie and I, had come. In 1964 and 1965 there are no visits recorded at all. These were the years leading up to our parents' divorce in November 1965, and it would seem that Bev had become a victim of their conflict.

Once the divorce was final and Dad was out of the house, Mother had no way to get to Pennhurst. Since she didn't drive she would have had to get someone else to take her. During this time Mother kept in touch with cards and letters, but apparently didn't see Bev at all. After the divorce, Dad visited just once in 1966 and once in 1967. Then came the letter from Pennhurst in August 1968 pleading for a visit. That letter did get a response from Dad who visited twice, once in September and once in December of 1968. After that, interest waned again, with only one visit in 1969 for Bev's birthday and another one in 1970. Two of his sign ins, however, listed two people visiting. The last notation on the visitors' card from Bev's cottage was made in April of 1970 showing a visit from Dad and a companion, but there is no indication who that other person might have been. Mother? A girlfriend? Me? Another interesting fact revealed by the file card is that between 1966 and 1970 Dad signed with four different addresses, all in the Reading area. Four moves in four years. In 1968 he rented a house only a few doors away from Mother. I'm sure she was delighted. Nevertheless, this little card reflects the turmoil of their breakup and its tragic results. It shows how little time they spent with Bev. They were preoccupied with their own lives, their own struggles. The reality of this time is that Bev was just not a priority. The divorce was the inevitable culmination of years of mistakes, bad judgment, lack of communication, selfishness, and denial. This was the stuff of our family dynamic. The five people who should have been the most responsible for Bev's welfare had, instead, let her down in so many ways.

Though all of us were adversely affected by the divorce, none was as profoundly affected as Bev. Like the rest of us Bev would have to grapple with loss and grief and uncertainty, but she lost so much more. From now on there would be no more family all in one house at one time. Indeed, there was no more real "home" for Bev anymore. Instead, for many years to come, there would be a stream of unfamiliar places and unfamiliar faces. The home Bev clung to in her memory was, in reality, gone forever. Nevertheless, even today she is sure that it still exists. She knows it like an old friend, and she carries it with her always.

~10~

The Winds of Change

Timing is everything and, unfortunately for Bev, her timing couldn't have been much worse. She was in the wrong place at the wrong time, born in an era when developmentally disabled children were considered "defectives" who needed to be isolated from normal people. When she was a little girl in need of community services for mentally handicapped children, there was almost nothing available to her. With mental health legislation and reforms still decades away, the accepted practice of placing intellectually disabled children in an institutional setting continued, and the population in public hospitals exploded. By the time Bev walked through its doors in 1952, Pennhurst State School was at its worst, bursting at the seams and admitting far more people than it could possibly serve. Bev was one of 700 people added to the rolls in the five years between 1950 and 1955, when the resident population jumped from 2800 to 3500. To make matters worse, not only was Pennhurst inhumanely overcrowded, it was also woefully understaffed and underfunded. This was institutionalization at its worst.

In truth Pennhurst was no different than dozens of other state hospitals like it throughout the country. All of the large public institutions had similar problems. In the 1960's, however, two things happened to change the fate of developmentally disabled children in the United States. First, great strides were made in the treatment of the intellectually disabled and mentally ill. The fields of psychology and psychiatry were burgeoning, while colleges and medical schools were turning out many more professionals trained in mental health care. New methods of diagnosis and treatment were being developed along with effective medications to aid in the management of emotional distress. To complement the medical advances, new techniques for educating cognitively disabled children and rehabilitating intellectually disabled adults were developed, and teachers trained in these methods began to enter the field. Second, while these medical and educational advances were taking place, the attitude of society towards the mentally challenged was also taking a new direction. No longer was the prevailing attitude one of protecting normal people from the "defectives." Intellectually disabled citizens were finally considered worthy of a happy and productive life, and the government began to enact legislation to protect and educate them. These events didn't occur overnight, but they did move rapidly once public awareness was turned toward the plight of the inmates of overflowing public residential institutions. As the winds of change began to blow, Pennhurst was swept along with them.

An important part of raising social awareness was the investigative reporting of journalists that took place during this time, especially on television. TV had progressed from a novel form of entertainment in the 1950's to the most influential agent of social change in the 1960's. Because of television millions of people were able to watch the civil rights movement unfold before their eyes. They gaped at the horrors of the Vietnam War on the nightly news. They were witnesses to assassination. TV was a powerful instrument that reporters began to use to keep the public informed about the pressing issues of the day, and one of those issues was the plight of the inmates of mental institutions. After decades in the shadows, this problem finally saw the light of day.

In the 1960's large state run institutions like Pennhurst started to come under the scrutiny of both politicians and the press. After John F. Kennedy was elected President in 1960 the issue of mental retardation came out of the closet when it was revealed that he himself had a mentally handicapped sister named Rosemary. Primarily because of her, the Kennedy family always had a personal interest in the plight of the mentally retarded. Eunice Kennedy Shriver worked tirelessly to champion mentally challenged citizens and spearheaded the nationalization of the Special Olympics in 1968. Her brother, Senator Robert Kennedy, also became involved when, in 1965, he toured New York's Willowbrook State Hospital, the largest state run institution of its kind in the United States. He was appalled at what he saw there, calling it a "snake pit" and declaring that zoo animals lived better than its inmates. This comparison to zoo animals crops up in other reports as well and seems to be a theme picked up by many advocates of mental health reform during that decade. Despite his comments and interest in improving conditions there, very little changed until seven years later, in 1972, when Willowbrook became the subject of a sensational television expose conducted by Geraldo Rivera. Rivera, then a reporter for WABC-TV in New York, did a series of reports called *Willowbrook: the Last Disgrace* that won him the Peabody Award and shocked the nation with its graphic footage of the deplorable conditions he uncovered.

Though Rivera garnered more national attention with his report on Willowbrook, Pennhurst had already had its ugly secret exposed four years earlier. In 1968 the spotlight fell on Pennhurst when Bill Baldini, a reporter for WCAU-TV in Philadelphia, travelled into the countryside about an hour from the city to produce a story about Pennhurst State School and Hospital. His report, titled "Suffer the Little Children," aired over five nights and exposed conditions at Pennhurst to national scrutiny. This report became a major influence on mental health reform not only in Pennsylvania but throughout the United States. The TV cameras showed disturbing images of disabled children and adults tied hand and foot in cribs and beds, patients wandering aimlessly in dreary day rooms and hallways, men sitting or lying half naked on the floor, ignored by everyone passing by. The images were stark and shocking. Baldini had conversations with some of the residents, trying to get their opinions on how they felt about living there. Their ability to respond was limited, but it was obvious that the newscaster was touched by their plight and wanted to see them free to live in the outside world.

Baldini also interviewed doctors, nurses, and other employees, who voiced their frustration over lack of funding and staffing. It was clear from listening to them that they were under a great deal of strain and that they were trying to do their best against overwhelming odds. At the time this report aired there were about 2800 residents at Pennhurst, yet there were just two psychiatrists and nine other doctors on staff. Although 900 of the residents were women, there was no staff gynecologist.

The Winds of Change

The educational programs in place could handle only about 200 children. There were eleven teachers, none with degrees in special education. Baldini made a stark financial comparison between Pennhurst and the Philadelphia Zoo. While the zoo was allocated $7.15 a day for each animal, Pennhurst was allocated a mere $5.90 a day for each patient. The animals at the zoo lived in cages far less crowded than the residential buildings on the Pennhurst campus. He made the point that, in our society, more value was placed on zoo animals than on mentally retarded human beings.

Needless to say, the facts and images in this landmark series of reports horrified viewers and caused a public outcry. It so happened at the time that there was a surplus of $40,000,000 in the state treasury. As a result of Baldini's report, some of that money was allocated to improve conditions at Pennhurst. After Baldini's exposé life inside Pennhurst would never be the same, but it was a classic case of too little too late. Despite changes and improvements within the system, the era of large institutions for the intellectually disabled and emotionally ill was coming to an end. For Pennhurst the end came swiftly. Twenty years after Baldini's report, Pennhurst was no more.

Although television exposes like Rivera's and Baldini's reached millions with their shocking images and emotional testimony, the printed word had its place in the revolution too. In 1966 a landmark photographic essay, *Christmas in Purgatory* by Burton Blatt, an educator and expert in the fields of special education and the rights of people with disabilities, was published in a limited edition and distributed to legislators, universities, and others actively involved in the administration of mental health services. The book, full of stark and disturbing photographs taken with a hidden camera, revealed the shocking conditions in the back wards of four unnamed public institutions for the intellectually disabled. The book was conceived not long after Bobby Kennedy's visits to several facilities for the mentally handicapped in New York State, including the infamous Willowbrook, which sparked public debate over the treatment of people with intellectual disabilities. Blatt wanted the book to be given to the people that he believed could enact change. Part of that change was legislation on both the federal and state level that could ensure the rights of people who were victimized by a flawed system in the realm of mental health.

All of these exposés and investigations in the media helped to push legislators to address this issue, and soon new laws were passed to protect, educate, and rehabilitate intellectually disabled citizens across the country. One of the most important pieces of legislation to affect Pennhurst was the Pennsylvania Mental Health and Retardation Act passed in 1966. When Pennhurst was forced to comply with the requirements of this act, significant changes began to take place there. The main goal of this act was to transfer the care and treatment of the intellectually disabled from large impersonal institutions to smaller, community based programs. It took almost twenty years, but ultimately that goal was met. To that end, one of the first tasks Pennhurst took on was improving living conditions on campus, by making renovations to the cottages as well as reducing the resident population to alleviate overcrowding. After 1966 the number of residents began to decline steadily, falling by over 1000 in just five years. During these renovations Bev was moved from unit to unit in the C complex, until she eventually moved to a totally different environment in Q building in 1970.

Another hugely important influence on Pennhurst was the creation of the Medicaid program in 1965. A joint venture between the federal and state governments, this program provides health care services for low income individuals. A Medicaid benefit created by the Social Security Act was called the ICF/MR (Intermediate Care Facilities for the Mentally Retarded). This part of the program allocated funds to facilities that provided "active treatment" for the mentally retarded. In order to receive these funds Pennhurst had to meet the guidelines that defined "active treatment". This requirement resulted in so many of the positive changes that came about at Pennhurst in the 1960's, including reduced client population, improved housing, increased staffing, and team based programming and organization. While ICF/MR revolutionized treatment for the mentally retarded in institutions, the national trend continued toward community living arrangements instead of institutionalization. In 1972 the Commonwealth of Pennsylvania established the Community Living Arrangements program with the goal of providing services for retarded citizens in small home settings within local communities and eliminating the need for large institutions like Pennhurst. A revolution for people with intellectual disabilities had finally begun.

In the 1960's the Pennsylvania Association for Retarded Citizens, which had actually existed since 1949, became involved in the history of Pennhurst. The goal of ARC was to do away with the institutionalization of retarded children completely. They advocated for the education of all children, regardless of intellectual abilities, in the public school system and sued the Commonwealth of Pennsylvania in 1971 to obtain that right for retarded children. That lawsuit eventually led to the passage of the federal Education for All Handicapped Children Act in 1975, which later evolved into the Individuals with Disabilities Education Act in 1990. These laws effectively made it possible for intellectually challenged children to remain at home with their families and attend their local schools. No longer were many parents forced to institutionalize children because they couldn't go to school. No longer did intellectually disabled children need to languish for lack of education and training.

It is interesting to note another significant change that came about gradually during these revolutionary times. The language used to refer to people with intellectual disabilities underwent a transformation. The names of organizations, agencies, and legislation began to drop the word "retarded". The word has continued to be used clinically, though even that is changing, but general use of that term is no longer considered appropriate. It also still has a place in a historical context, because that is the word that was used for many decades to replace "feebleminded" to describe people with intellectual and developmental disabilities. It is the word I grew up hearing and using, and so it has become part of my history and my perspective.

Unfortunately, the revolution came too late for Bev. Her childhood had passed by and been wasted. By the time Bill Baldini stood outside the overcrowded brick fortress of Pennhurst with his cameras and microphone, Bev was 25 years old. The malleable young girl of nine had been replaced by a mentally and physically battered young woman who had been inside those walls for 16 long years. There was no going back to retrieve that little girl, yet there was hope. She would remain at Pennhurst for 16 more years and, although she bore the scars of battle, the second half of her life there would be very different from the first half. She was a survivor who set sail on those winds of change to a second chance at life.

~11~

The Brown Notebook

The letters home to our parents from the staff in the 1970's reflected the positive new direction Bev's life was taking at Pennhurst. They were always upbeat as they focused on the new efforts at education, both academic and behavioral, on the opportunities for interaction with the community, and on enrichment activities like swimming, sports, art and music. Just like notes sent home from an elementary school teacher, they were intended to make the parents feel good about their children and to encourage them to take an active part in their education. After years of formality and secrecy, this was a totally new approach. It was very challenging for parents to adapt to the new policies, and it was often an uphill battle for the social workers to get families involved with relatives whom they had considered hopelessly lost in every sense. Many families didn't want to get involved and some families, like ours, simply didn't know how. These new programs shook up everyone's world.

While the letters sent home to our parents were unfailingly positive, the daily logs and statistical records kept by the social workers and other staff show another side of managing and educating a intellectually disabled adult who had been neglected by the system for so long, and who still functioned as a child. The doctors, social workers, and aides worked diligently every day to implement new approaches to treating the intellectually disabled. It was a time of innovation, and even experimentation, as staff entered uncharted territory. The methods were not always gentle or kind, but they eventually produced results and gave renewed hope to the hopeless. In compliance with progressive state regulations, beginning in the 1970's, detailed records were kept for all patients. Daily interaction with Bev was monitored and recorded, and every health issue, behavioral modification attempt, and medication was carefully documented.

Buried among the records in Bev's Pennhurst file is a small brown essay notebook used as a log for attendants who looked after Bev. The notebook covers a period from August 1970 to January 1972. Why this particular notebook was included in her files, I don't know. Was it one of many that just happened to survive? Was it an experiment that was abandoned? Whatever the case, it is a fascinating and revealing narrative of Bev's everyday life during that year and a half. The entries in the notebook are handwritten, and the first thing I noticed was how often the handwriting changed. Each entry was initialed, and I counted seventeen different writers. This reflects not only shift rotation, but a fairly regular turnover in staff. How difficult it must have been for anyone to make any progress in getting to know an individual resident. One of the aides talks about wanting to get to know Bev better so that she could try to get through to her and help her, but her entries were in the book for only five months. Toward the end of the notebook there was another person whose notes regularly appeared for about nine months until all entries simply stopped abruptly on January 17, 1972. There is no explanation as to why the log was discontinued at that point and no indication that they were going to end. The final entry states "Right now she [sic] still in the hole screaming 3:20".

The attendants whose entries appear in the notebook apparently were following a protocol designed specifically for Bev. They had been taught to use various positive and negative reinforcements at regular intervals to shape Bev's behavior. These aides obviously read each other's notes to keep abreast of Bev's progress. A supervising psychologist also read the log periodically, jotting down comments in the margins and providing ongoing guidance and training to the aides. Overall the aides seemed dedicated and tried their best to implement the program even if they weren't always convinced it was the best approach. They had their work cut out for them, because dealing with Bev was like riding a roller coaster. She seemed to have periods when she was docile and cooperative, but then, without warning, she would turn into a wild woman. In the very beginning of the notebook one aide expressed her reaction to this type of behavior.

> I do believe I stepped in over my head when I volunteered to take Beverly as my primary assignment. Why? I'm scared to death of her. One back hand from Miss Miller would send me flying across the room, so, as a result, I find myself appeasing her rather than 'programing' [sic] her.

Bev had always had a violent side which had sometimes intimidated her family as well. The tantrums she had exhibited as a child later became dangerous outbursts. These episodes were one of the reasons she had stopped coming home for extended family visits. Once she grew big enough to do real damage, she was a force to be reckoned with. By the late 1970's she was grossly overweight, close to 200 pounds. We used to joke that she could be a linebacker for the Philadelphia Eagles. However, if you had to deal with her when she was angry, it was no joke. Bev could often lash out with hitting, biting, scratching, and spitting at both staff and other residents. One of her favorite assaults was pinching. Even today she will pinch lightly and say "pinchy, pinchy", but these days we make sure that she keeps the pinches playfully gentle. Since combativeness among residents at Pennhurst was not unusual, and injuries often resulted, Bev had to learn to defend herself early on. She was incredibly strong, and once she found that she could scare people, she used that fear to get her way. It took a brave aide to try to discipline her.

Bev's negative behavior took many forms. Besides assaulting people, she also soiled herself and peed on the floor, tore her clothing, used foul language, threw furniture, broke windows, screamed and cried, stole food, performed somersaults, and banged her head against the walls. Banging her head against walls was something that the aides tried hard to prevent but with little success. All Bev's rage and frustration was vented through her head banging episodes. For years she sported bruises and cuts, some needing stitches, and she still bears scars and lumps from those old injuries. Though staff tried hard to keep her from hurting herself, it was almost impossible. In the early days of her residence they used a straight jacket, euphemistically called a "camisole". Later, there were muff shackles and other similar restraints. But in the latter years they tried to refrain from using restraints as they attempted to mold her behavior and fade out her old coping mechanisms. Sometimes isolation helped calm her. Injections, usually seconal, were given to quiet her when all else failed. Bev herself would sometimes say, "Gimmee a shot," when she knew she was out of control.

Both negative and positive reinforcements were part of Bev's program. When a caseworker from Pennhurst made a home visit to Mother's house to explain the program to her, Dad was there also. Before this program was started, both Mother and Dad signed a Special Treatment Authorization document that gave permission to the staff to use certain negative reinforcements. Both of them signed it, an unusual collaboration for them, as they managed to put aside their differences for awhile to help in Bev's renaissance. The document they signed authorized some extreme measures, but they realized that it was necessary to use such techniques to get results. For the first time in many years they had some hope that Bev could learn to live a productive life. Whatever problems they had in their own relationship, they were still Bev's parents, and they wanted to do what was right for her sake. They gladly gave the social workers and psychologists the green light to do what had to be done.

Some of the negative practices used in her program were isolation, rubbing food in her face, holding her down on the floor, and forcing her to kneel in a corner facing the wall. One form of isolation was a place called "the hole" where Bev was placed for short periods to calm down. At times Bev recognized on her own that she needed to sit in the corner or go into "the hole", and sometimes she actually went there voluntarily. To reward good behavior Bev was allowed to wear a wig and sunglasses (quite a sight to behold), have her fingernails polished, or carry a pocketbook. She also received rewards of candy or cookies and, later, earned tokens that she used to buy sweets. When well behaved she could also go outside for walks or attend movies with other residents. One of her regular repetitive phrases is still "no movies tonight." Those behavior modification techniques used almost forty years ago obviously made quite an impression on her.

The prevailing policy with Bev seemed to be to try to talk her out of her disturbed periods. If that didn't work, positive reinforcement was withheld, and if that didn't work, negative reinforcement was used. In one entry the attendant expressed the opinion that Bev needed less talk and more punishment. The psychologist made a note suggesting that the person who wrote that comment didn't understand the program. That was the first and last entry made by that particular aide, who was probably transferred elsewhere. Everyone was expected to follow the program whether he or she agreed with it or not. The aides who wrote the notes were conscientious, for the most part, and really seemed to try to help Bev. When she was being good, they enjoyed being with her. When she was being bad, they not only had to endure being hit and screamed at, but they had to clean up after her when she wet herself, and get her fresh clothes when she tore them off. Bev had periods when she was wonderful, but she also had periods when she was a demon. The frustrating part for the staff was that there just didn't seem to be any pattern to her moods. No one could figure out what set her off. There were certain triggers - going outside onto the grounds, too much stimulation from other patients who were boisterous or noisy, teasing by fellow residents, or being denied treats when she was on a diet. But for the most part her moods followed no discernible pattern and triggers were not always predictable. Bev was a mystery that they couldn't seem to solve.

When I was reading this notebook, I came to some conclusions of my own about Bev's behavior. This is only my opinion, formed by reading reports on her patterns of behavior alongside her medical records. The brown notebook describes in detail Bev's violent behaviors like head banging, biting, hitting, and even smashing windows. I can't help wondering if some of Bev's worst behavior was triggered by physical problems. For instance, she had a prolapsed rectum during this time that wasn't repaired until ten years later in 1981. That condition certainly must have caused her great discomfort and anxiety. Why was it ignored for so long? She also was plagued with gastrointestinal problems for her entire adult life. Who knows how often she had an upset stomach? She was hospitalized with gastroenteritis in 1971 after having been sick to her stomach off and on for over two months. During this time of stomach problems she also fell down some stairs and hurt her knee, after which she spent all day crying and sleeping. When her behavior became so bad in the following days that she needed calming injections, one of the aides suggested that her "going off" may have been caused by her not feeling well. It seems a logical conclusion. One thing that no one ever mentions is the fact that Bev was very nearsighted all her life. As a child she wore eyeglasses, but at Pennhurst she never had them. Not being able to see more than a few feet ahead of her certainly could have caused some anxiety and confusion as well as the inability to follow directions. I think her poor eyesight would certainly have affected her ability to function in the classroom and could help explain why she failed at the little schooling Pennhurst provided when she was younger. Bev also often complained about toothache. Her teeth had become decayed and certainly caused her pain. They were all finally removed in 1967, but afterwards she may have had some sort of pain or soreness in her gums or jaw. Everyone dismissed her complaints because she had no teeth, but even eating without teeth could cause sore gums. She also still had her menstrual periods at this time. Did she have cramps and PMS? What about her head banging? Did she have headaches, even migraines? Or earaches? Did she have tinnitus? I don't see records of anyone looking for physical reasons for her behavior other than urology tests to explain her lack of bladder control.

Another thing that also certainly affected her behavior was the fact that because of her obesity, she was continually placed on various diets. Food was very important to Bev, and being constantly hungry can make anyone miserable. She repeatedly got in trouble for stealing food. She was disciplined by having food rubbed in her face and was made to sit in front of plates of food without touching it. Who could blame her for feeling angry and frustrated? To make matters worse, one of her main rewards for good behavior was candy or cookies. When she was on a diet, the aides cut back on her treats. Bev got really mad when food was withheld from her and responded by hitting staff when they wouldn't give her a treat. They eventually came up with other rewards like painting her fingernails or letting her carry a pocketbook, but Bev always considered food her primary payoff.

We will never know exactly how Bev's physical health affected her mental state. Since she didn't have the verbal capacity to clearly explain what was bothering her, it would have taken a lot of testing and questioning and examining to get to the bottom of her physical discomfort. I believe a lot of physical problems were probably disregarded because of her mental disability, and that her behavior could certainly have been affected by any one of them. As a case in point, she recently went through a period when she was lethargic and had trouble concentrating. Staff began to believe that serious dementia was setting in. It took a long time to figure it out, but eventually she was diagnosed with Type II diabetes. Once she was placed on a strict low carb diet, her energy level went up and the signs of dementia she was displaying lessened considerably. It is a perfect example of how her physical condition affected her mental state and behavior. I truly believe that some of her past maladaptive behavior was caused, or made worse, by her physical ailments.

The new behavioral modification program documented in the brown notebook was begun in August 1970, and though the daily log listed many negative episodes, there was obviously progress in Bev's overall behavior. By 1971 she began to participate in activities off the Pennhurst grounds. According to the notes, her first such outing was an all day excursion in January of that year. The psychologist assigned to her unit took her into town where they went shopping and ate lunch in a local restaurant. If this trip was a test to see how Bev would do outside in the real world, she apparently passed with flying colors. The psychologist reported that both she and Bev had a great time and Bev was very well behaved all afternoon. Bev loved the car ride, and the newfound freedom it brought, and didn't want to return at the end of the day. She earned her wings during that outing and, as time went on, was able to participate in many more similar excursions to nearby towns and shopping malls.

The staff was so pleased with the outcome that they wrote a letter home to Mother and Dad to let them know what a success the outing had been. It was a significant event that became a turning point for Bev. Following this success Bev started to take part in other activities like going to a pool for swimming lessons, which began a lifelong love of being in the water. These were the first giant steps toward her future independence. One of the best results of her newfound self control was yet to come. Even though Bev was still having behavior issues, she apparently had improved enough to enter a new stage of treatment, and she started to attend school again for the first time in many years.

Nevertheless, a consistent theme of all the entries in the notebook was the erratic nature of Bev's behavior. It was entirely unpredictable, going from angelic to demonic in a matter of minutes, even seconds. When she was upset Bev struck out at everyone, male and female alike, with stronger males called on to handle her when she was seriously out of control. During the year and a half that entries were made in this notebook, Bev was given calming injections and put in seclusion on a regular basis. Although the program called for positive and negative reinforcements and the staff tried to talk Bev down from her rampages, there were times when, for both Bev's and the staff's safety, Bev needed to be subdued with drugs or seclusion or even shackles. The sedative injections she was given not only helped the staff to deal with her agitation, but also made Bev herself feel so much better. After she had been given an injection she went to sleep and usually woke feeling much calmer and more relaxed. Because no amount of behavior modification was ever going to eliminate the need for drugs in Bev's therapy, finding the right drugs and the right levels of medication would become key to her recovery.

After the brown notebook was discontinued, detailed records were still kept daily throughout the 1970's and '80's, but the notations were contained in large binders on forms that provided only a few cramped lines to write on. The more informal format of the brown essay notebook had encouraged the writers to make longer entries with more subjective observations, and the personalities of the staff shone through as they made their comments on Bev's behavior and activities. As a matter of fact, Bev had formed a special relationship with one of the female aides whose entries appear there. The aide's notes reflect her affection and it's obvious that she really likes Bev. She sometimes calls her a "good little girl" or a "nice little lady" when she's behaving well. She tried to figure out why Bev "went off" and did everything she could think of to calm her and redirect her. Occasionally Bev would hit her, which genuinely hurt her feelings. Although Bev hit many of the staff, this particular aide felt that she had a special rapport with Bev that was betrayed when she hit her, but, even so, she went out of her way to add that Bev never hit her very hard. This close relationship must have continued for some time because it was mentioned years later in a caseworker's report prior to Bev's consideration for a community living arrangement.

Of all the comments made throughout the brown notebook, one struck me as particularly significant. In April of 1971, just before Easter, one of the aides wrote that Bev's parents were coming to visit her and writes, "Should prove interesting!" What could have prompted her to she say that? The nature of that statement leads me to believe that visits were not a common occurrence. In fact, this is the only time a visit is mentioned in the one and a half year period that the notebook covers. The day of the visit the entry says that "her family" came, and that appears to be the truth. It was almost the whole family, not just

her parents. I unearthed a photograph that I believe depicts that particular visit. It shows not only Mother and Dad, but also Greg and his wife Chris, their two little girls, me, and my husband (then boyfriend) Greg. Bev is sitting with an Easter basket filled with black jelly beans, her favorite, and a stuffed rabbit. Her head is shaved and there is an ugly cut on her forehead. Although she isn't smiling, Bev looks fairly contented and calm. The rest of us are all smiling broadly and trying to make it a festive event. The entry in the log afterwards says that Bev seemed to enjoy our company and was upset when we left. The comments of the aides seem to indicate that visitations were, indeed, infrequent, and that this visit was obviously a special event. I believe it was the result of our parents' new attempts at cooperation, which were aided and encouraged by our brother Greg and his wife. However it came about, it ushered in an era of more family participation in Bev's life than had taken place in a very long time.

Out of all the other documents I uncovered in my research of Bev's Pennhurst records, this little brown notebook provided me with the most intimate look into Bev's life at Pennhurst. To hear the narrative from the people who worked so closely with her on a day to day basis showed me a side of her that I could never see in the professional evaluations and jargon from other reports. The notebook entries, however, lasted only a year and a half and ended abruptly in January 1972. In that same month our parents received a letter informing them that there was a newly revised behavior modification program being put in place in Unit VIII where Bev was residing. Once the new program was begun and the little brown notebook was no longer used, daily records were kept in a different format and lost their intimacy. Although the notebook's log ended abruptly with Bev still screaming in "the hole," she had made significant progress during those years. Her overall behavior had improved, and she was back in school and performing well. She still had a very long way to go, but she was on her way up in the world, and each passing day took her closer to a new and better life.

~12~

The Endgame

In 1974, a remarkable event occurred that turned the mental health community on its head. The parents of Pennhurst resident Terri Lee Halderman filed a lawsuit against Pennhurst alleging that their residents were forced to live in conditions of demeaning neglect and abuse. While several other residents joined Terri as plaintiffs, dozens of other residents, including Bev, were represented by the Parents and Family Association of Pennhurst, which had been organized in 1967. Beverley Lynne Miller had become part of the landmark Halderman v. Pennhurst State School and Hospital, a class action lawsuit on behalf of retarded citizens, brought before U.S. District Judge Raymond J. Broderick.

It is ironic that by the time the lawsuit was filed, conditions at Pennhurst had already begun to improve, albeit slowly and still without adequate staff or funding. The resident population, for example, which had reached its peak in 1955 at about 3500 had been reduced to about 1600 by 1974 when the lawsuit was begun. New procedures and programs had been put in place by the mid 1960's and residents were receiving more individual attention. The conditions described in the testimony given during the trial, horrific as they sounded, were actually better than they had been years earlier. Twelve year old Terri Lee Halderman became a resident of Pennhurst in 1966, at a time when reforms had already begun. Yet, after years of watching their daughter decline, just as Bev and most other patients had, her parents decided to sue the institution responsible for her suffering and deterioration. They were demanding that conditions at Pennhurst be improved dramatically.

The passage of the Pennsylvania Mental Health and Retardation Act in 1966 had already started a statewide trend toward community living arrangements rather than institutionalization. Even so, the large institutions were still full and in need of money to provide for their residents. Two years later, in 1968, Bill Baldini's disturbing TV report brought public attention to the problems at Pennhurst and was instrumental in helping acquire the necessary increase in state funding. The progressive reforms at Pennhurst didn't happen overnight. It took years for the new programs to be implemented. Even when the programs were adopted, it was obvious that it was going to take much more time to undo the damage done over the previous decades.

A patient like Bev, with her severe problems, needed intense rehabilitation. It took a lot of vision to see that someone like her could ever reclaim her life. Her psychological evaluation in 1966 says that she was "classified as being an overactive and dangerous patient." She had fallen so far that she was now a danger to herself and others. Because of her uncontrollable behavior, she had long since been excluded from any group activities or training programs, but it was time for that to change. A new era was beginning for Bev. She was finally going to receive the kind of treatment that would eventually allow her to participate in the educational and life skills classes that were slowly transforming the residents' lives. But the changes weren't happening fast enough, and someone finally decided to do something about it. That someone was the Halderman family.

Whether our parents were offered the opportunity to testify in court, I don't know. Other patients or their family members did testify about their personal experiences at the institution, revealing their own details of neglect or abuse and degrading living conditions. Bev was not verbal enough to have been able to testify, and, knowing my mother, I'm sure that even if she were presented with that choice, she would definitely have declined it. Besides the fact that she would never have wanted the public attention it would have brought, she would not have wanted to face describing what her daughter had gone through at Pennhurst. I believe that the only way Mother survived the ordeal of having Bev at Pennhurst was by shutting out the reality. By the time Halderman vs. Pennhurst was initiated, Bev had already been a Pennhurst resident for over 20 years. I am sure that our parents had no hope that she would ever leave, that she would ever have any other life. In 1974 they would never have believed that in ten years time Bev would leave Pennhurst forever and that, soon after, Pennhurst would be no more.

During the trial, the testimony of the plaintiffs in the case revealed examples of overcrowding, neglect, and abuse that shocked the judge. Even the depositions from Superintendent C. Duane Youngberg and other administrative staff corroborated the bleak picture painted by the residents and their families. The facts and figures now had names and faces and voices attached to them. The words "under staffed", "over crowded", and "under funded" now had new meaning. Those words defined the lives of the disabled citizens who lived at Pennhurst State School and Hospital. The results of those words were described in heartbreaking detail.

The dark picture of Pennhurst painted at the trial began with the physical environment itself. Through the years the buildings had become rundown, with damage from leaky roofs, missing railings, cracked windows, and crumbling concrete. Paint peeled, plaster cracked, plumbing didn't work. In many bathrooms there were broken toilets and faucets, and there was often no soap or toilet paper. Some buildings actually had no hot water, which naturally led to poor sanitation. The staff couldn't possibly keep the buildings clean. Floors and walls were often smeared with urine and feces. Noxious odors wafted through the rooms and hallways. Needless to say, because of such unsanitary conditions, outbreaks of disease, worms, and skin ailments were common. Patients sometimes walked about naked because staff had no time to change their clothes when they soiled them or tore them off. The noise level in day rooms was often so loud that conversation was impossible and some patients simply stopped speaking altogether. Instead, they wailed and moaned and screamed, or merely rocked silently. The constant noise agitated many patients and drove them to lose control.

As a result of the overcrowding and insufficient staff, violence was an unavoidable part of daily life at Pennhurst. Residents often assaulted each other or started fights. Injuries ranged from bruises, black eyes, scratches, bite marks, and lost teeth to broken bones, serious lacerations, blindness, and even death. In January 1977, for instance, 833 minor injuries and 25 serious injuries were reported. Aides also were sometimes injured on the wards, either by outright attacks or as a result of restraining a disturbed patient. In their attempts to defend themselves, to control a violent outburst, or perhaps even in their own frustration or anger, they also sometimes inflicted physical harm on residents. In their attempts to control dangerous and self abusive behaviors, staff used several types of restraints. Sometimes they used physical restraints such as straightjackets or shackles, euphemistically referred to as camisoles and muffs. Many patients were tied to chairs, beds, or benches or bound in wheelchairs. Some residents spent hours in seclusion rooms. When seclusion and restraints failed, drugs like seconal, mellaril, and thorazine were given as sedatives.

In addition to actual physical confrontations that could result in injuries, accidents were also rampant. With so many people to watch, it was impossible for staff to supervise patients properly. Residents roaming about at will often fell down stairs, smashed their hands through windows, barreled into doors or collided with other people. Outdoors many residents were left to wander the grounds unattended. Tragically, in July 1974, two such unsupervised residents went off on their own and drowned in the nearby Schuylkill River.

In response to the chaos, boredom, and lack of meaningful interaction, many patients developed maladaptive behaviors ranging from hitting and biting to rocking and pacing to head banging and self abuse. Almost all of them regressed after arriving at Pennhurst, losing many of the skills and abilities they had when they were admitted. Some forgot their toilet training and lost the ability to control their bowels and bladders, which resulted in urine and feces smeared on walls, floors, and each other. Their physical health suffered from lack of activity, poor diet, unsanitary conditions, infectious diseases, and injuries. For the majority of residents, not only did they not improve while they lived at Pennhurst, they became much worse.

Who would voluntarily want to live in such conditions? Yet, technically, the residents were there voluntarily. All residents over 18 were informed that they could leave the institution. However, if they weren't able to understand that they had alternatives or they couldn't communicate their wishes, it was assumed that they wanted to stay where they were. In truth, alternatives were few and far between, especially for the more severely mentally or physically handicapped. The cruel fact was that most of the parents who admitted their children to Pennhurst did so because there were no alternatives. Placing their children at Pennhurst was a last resort because there were no programs in their communities to help them educate and care for their handicapped children. That certainly was the case for Bev. There simply was nowhere else to go.

We take for granted today that public schools will educate all children, but that wasn't the case until a national right to education law was passed in 1974. This law was passed primarily as a result of a lawsuit filed by the Pennsylvania Association for Retarded Citizens in 1971, a reaction to the conditions at Pennhurst and the plight of the children who were sent there only because they could not attend public school. The lawsuit, filed against the State of Pennsylvania, sought to get access to public education for all children. This suit was settled in a consent decree establishing the right of children with intellectual disabilities to attend public schools. This decree became the model for the EHA (Education for All Handicapped Children Act) in 1974, which evolved into the IDEA (Individuals with Disabilities Education Act) in place today. With guaranteed education and improved social services, most parents these days are able to keep their children at home with their families so that they can live with their siblings and attend public school in inclusive classrooms. The situation is far from ideal, and parents still have daunting challenges, but it is a far cry from what people faced when Bev was a little girl.

It was in March of 1978, at the conclusion of the Halderman v. Pennhurst lawsuit, that a court order was issued by Judge Raymond Broderick. This court order addressed all of the terrible conditions at Pennhurst, outlining in detail the steps that needed to be taken to alleviate those conditions and arranging for a "special master" to be appointed to oversee the process. As a result new policies were put in place at Pennhurst by a new superintendent, and all employees received training and instruction on how to interact with the patients following the court ordered guidelines. Perhaps the most radical provision of Judge Broderick's order was that all residents of Pennhurst must eventually be removed from the institution into community living arrangements. Though the Commonwealth of Pennsylvania appealed that decision, proposing that some patients needed to remain in an institutional setting, the original decision prevailed and all Pennhurst residents found living situations within the community. Ironically, Terri Halderman's parents never intended for Pennhurst to close. They only wanted their daughter's living conditions at Pennhurst to improve. In the end Pennhurst was deemed beyond fixing. It was doomed.

Because of the court's ruling, Bev was designated as one of the individuals to be moved out of Pennhurst. The process of moving patients out was a huge undertaking, and it would be a long time before Bev actually left. First, individuals like her needed to be taught how to live in a "normal" environment after so many years in an institution. In addition, Community Living Arrangements had to be established to receive the newly discharged residents. All of this required finding suitable housing, training staff, and establishing partnerships with community organizations which would provide support services. Though the final court decision came down in 1979, Bev herself remained at Pennhurst until 1984. When she finally did leave she was one of only 400 individuals who still resided at Pennhurst. In the end, all residents were placed in some sort of community living arrangement. It was over. In 1987 Pennhurst was closed forever.

Bev had now become part of history. The Halderman v. Pennhurst State School was a landmark case that eventually made its way to the Supreme Court of the United States. It had far reaching effects on the landscape of mental health care in this country. After the lawsuit, Pennhurst became the focal point for a revolution in the care of the intellectually disabled, not only in Pennsylvania, but throughout the entire Country. By shining the light on the conditions at Pennhurst, the Halderman lawsuit precipitated long overdue reform, and the 1970's became a decade of progress in the treatment and housing of intellectually disabled people in the United States. For Bev and others of her generation it was a "better late than never" scenario, but at least their suffering was not in vain. As they left the confines of Pennhurst to live in community settings, these brave survivors led the way into a better world for the generations who would follow.

~13~

Opening the Door

As the case of Halderman v. Pennhurst State School dragged on throughout much of the 1970's, conditions at Pennhurst continued to improve. In the end, however, after the court decided that the institution should be closed, the main emphasis at Pennhurst shifted to moving its residents elsewhere. The first step was to evaluate each client to determine what kind of living arrangements were appropriate. Could she live on her own in an apartment? If so, how much supervision did she require? Was a group home a better choice? Could she hold a job? What was the status of her health? Did she have physical as well as mental handicaps? All of these questions and more needed to be answered and addressed. Retraining staff was a priority as programs were improved or expanded. The residents needed to be educated in personal hygiene and safety, and to learn the skills necessary to live in a home environment, everything from dressing themselves to making their beds to fixing a meal. Those capable of learning to read and write and count also needed to attend school. Meanwhile, outside in the community, apartments and houses needed to be located, staff hired and trained to supervise mentally intellectually disabled adults, organizations expanded, or even newly created, to coordinate the care of their clients. Mountains of forms needed to be filled out and new guidelines followed to the letter of the law. Funds needed to be allocated and administered. A system of health care providers had to be formed. It was a monumental

114

task, and it took years to make it all happen.

Depending on their level of retardation, it took months, or even years, to prepare Pennnurst's residents to live outside the institution. After so many years of mere warehousing, it was like waking them from a long sleep induced by a wicked witch in a fairytale. It was during this period of sweeping change that Bev's journey to freedom actually began. Because of the court's decision in the lawsuit, Bev was guaranteed support by the Commonwealth of Pennsylvania in a community setting for the rest of her life. She had already been moved into the Independence Unit, a modular cluster set up with the atmosphere of a group home. There Pennhurst residents were able to live more independently in preparation for a move into the community. As early as the spring of 1979, Bev was being considered for a Community Living Arrangement, but since there were not enough group homes available in Berks County, she had nowhere to go. It would be late in 1983 before a suitable residence could be found for her. In the meantime, she continued her metamorphosis within the confines of Pennhurst.

From the beginning, the residential buildings at Pennhurst had been quaintly called "cottages." To most people that word evokes images of cozy little bungalows, but in this case it merely meant designated living areas. Residents lived in utilitarian brick buildings filled with overcrowded, smelly, joyless rooms. In the early days they had the look of hospital wards with rows of beds and almost no other furniture. What few personal possessions people had were kept locked away to avoid loss or theft. However, when in 1968 the Commonwealth of Pennsylvania released additional funds for Pennhurst to improve its living conditions, the buildings were repaired and updated, attempts were made to make the interiors look more homey, and the atmosphere of confinement was reduced. Along with the physical changes came new educational and behavioral programs, and each building was divided into units according to the type of program in place there.

From the time Bev was admitted to Pennhurst in 1952 until 1970, she had lived in the C cottages, but late in 1970 she made the move to Q Building, later called Quaker Hall. She was assigned to Unit VIII where teams comprised of a social worker, a psychologist, and support staff implemented structured programs in an attempt to help some of the most seriously challenged residents overcome their maladaptive behav-

iors and become more independent individuals. This is where she started the program of individualized behavior modification described in the
brown notebook, and this is when Bev began to bloom. As her behavior began to improve, she attended school again, but she was like a first
grader who had missed 2160 days of school. The nine year old girl who
came to Pennhurst in 1952 had never had a chance to grow up. In 1970,
at the age of 27, she had a lot of catching up to do. Even though her
mental age might never surpass that of a six year old child, she somehow
had to learn the life skills of an adult. That was the challenge that faced
the staff of Q-2, Unit VIII.

To meet that challenge, the first thing the staff had to tackle was
Bev's behavior. In order for Bev to be able to learn anything, she first
needed to get control of herself. The maladaptive behaviors that she
had developed in the chaotic institutional environment had to go. By far
her most dangerous behavior was banging her head against walls and
floors. It was her most deeply ingrained behavior and the hardest to
erase. For years her scalp was so bruised and lacerated that, with her
buzz cut hair and battered face, she resembled an unlucky prize fighter.
To this day the lumps and scars on her head and face are a record of her
self abusive behavior. Eventually, through behavioral modification and
proper medication, her head banging all but disappeared from her daily
routine, but even forty years later, if her medications become unbalanced
or she is emotionally stressed, she will return to it like an old friend.

Bev was not only self-abusive, but could also be violent toward others, and her prize fighter appearance sometimes matched her combative
attitude. Unfortunately, there were times when she became so disturbed
and out of control, that isolating her was the only alternative. The
brown notebook that aides used to record Bev's daily behavior in 1970
and '71 reveals the use of isolation or sedating injections as the only way
to calm her down. Through the years her childhood tantrums had
evolved into dangerous, explosive episodes. This behavior, like the head
banging, eventually faded, even though it still lurks below the surface of
her medications and is always in danger of erupting under stressful circumstances.

Some of her other maladaptive behaviors included rocking, pacing,
twirling, whining, repetitive speech, hair pulling and twisting, nail biting,
over eating, and stealing, (which was really a hoarding impulse), as well
as obsessive/compulsive actions like tapping or kissing objects, walls

and floors. Her relationship with food had also become obsessive and resulted in her becoming grossly overweight. Her list of food preferences has always been one of her main topics of conversation. For Bev food represents not only enjoyment but also comfort and approval. It had always been used as a reward for good behavior. That's one of the reasons she became obese. When Bev was eating, she was happy. Sweet treats were given to her for following directions and staying calm. When she became more independent she could earn tokens to spend at the canteen where she bought soft drinks and candy. As a result, Bev became heavier and heavier. Though her weight eventually became a serious health issue, she didn't really slim down until years after she left the institutional environment.

Once Bev's maladaptive behaviors faded she was able to concentrate on learning and communicating. Part of her training centered on two way communication. Bev has never developed the ability to engage in a true give and take conversation, but she was able to learn how to respond appropriately to verbal prompts directed to her by other people. Once she could do that, she started to master life skills. She learned how to dress herself, bathe, brush her teeth, toilet herself, make her bed, take care of personal possessions, help do simple chores, go from one place to another on the campus by herself, even ride a bus - all the skills she would need to live a "normal" life. She was also able to begin occupational therapy that would help her work in a sheltered workshop someday. Even though all these wonderful changes were coming about, life at Pennhurst was still no bowl of cherries for Bev. Her program included some very tough love. Our parents had already given permission for the staff to use some rather harsh negative reinforcements, such as having food rubbed in her face or kneeling in a corner facing the wall. But this behavior modification plan, combined with Bev's move to Q - 2, was the true beginning of Bev's renaissance.

During this time, our parents entered into a period of detente in order to help Bev succeed in her new program. Their new attitude of collaboration was a very significant development, because after the divorce their relationship had completely fallen apart, with both of them feeling hurt and bitter. By 1970 they had been divorced for five years and had moved on with new partners and new lives. Our mother was particularly defensive and cautious when it came to her relationship with her ex-husband. She dealt with her pain by remaining aloof and interacting with him as little as possible. However, even though their partnership was far from warm, they were able to get together as parents and do what was best for their child. They each received letters from the social workers at Pennhurst, giving them information on programs and activities that Bev was participating in and updating them on Bev's health issues. They both signed permission slips at various times for Bev's participation in certain activities, as well as several admissions to the hospital for tests and treatment.

Unfortunately, despite their increased involvement, Bev needed more from both of them. Throughout her adult years, the lack of parental visits had been a consistent problem for her. While our parents were still together, and she was young, they made sure to see her fairly regularly. Once they split up, however, Bev became collateral damage in the breakup. Even though by the time of the divorce she was 22 years old, she was mentally still a child and needed her parents as much as she ever had. The post divorce neglect turned out to be at the root of much of the disturbed and abusive behavior that was undermining her progress.

Teasing from her fellow residents was often the trigger for violent episodes, and her desire to go home hampered her ability to function in the environment at Pennhurst or to benefit from her behavioral modification programs. Bev's annual program review in August of 1975 states clearly addresses this issue: "Beverly becomes upset when other residents tease her and tell her, her mother will not come for a visit. At other times especially during holidays, she works herself up into a snit thinking about visits and she will then become abusive." In October of the following year, her annual review contains this comment: "Beverly is extremely attached to her family. Their failure to visit her as often as she would like, especially around the holidays, leads to periods of hyperactivity and aggression."

From the day she first set foot in Pennhurst, Bev had obsessed about going home. Nothing was more important to her. Through the years her visits with her family, either at home or at Pennhurst, were all she lived for. Ironically, though family meant everything to her, our family was never what you would call close-knit. As time went on, the gaps between us grew wide and deep. Once all of us children were adults, we and our parents should have discussed Bev's needs and come up with some sort of schedule to make sure that she never went for months without seeing anyone. Sadly, our family didn't operate that way. All of us could have made more of a concerted effort to send her cards and letters in between visits. Instead, the truth is that Mother was the only one who ever did that. Attention paid to Bev was hit or miss. Quite frankly, the rest of us didn't pay all that much attention to each other either. Bev was the innocent victim of our family's general disengagement, and her six-year-old mind wasn't able to cope with it. It made her time at Pennhurst a lonely and frustrating confinement.

Despite limited family involvement, with the intense program on Unit VIII, Bev began to improve and even thrive. By 1974 Bev was doing so well that the director of the unit felt that she was ready to transfer to a less restrictive unit. For most of that year she had been participating in activities designed to give residents a variety of off ward experiences in a unit called Exit House, where she learned skills like helping to prepare food, setting a table, and doing light house cleaning. In a classroom setting she worked on writing the alphabet and printing her full name. She also found out that she had a creative side which she expressed through artwork and crafts like painting, drawing, and embroidery. Her physical activities included swimming lessons, which she has always loved. At Exit House she had her hair washed and set and her fingernails polished. She was able to go on group trips to a nearby Japanese garden, to historical Valley Forge, and to shopping malls. She even went on an overnight camping trip. These experiences meant a great deal to her. She never forgot them and, for years afterward, talked excitedly about going to Valley Forge. During this time she was so well behaved, and did so well at all her activities, that it was determined that she no longer needed the intense and restrictive program in Unit VIII.

The problem facing the staff was deciding which unit to move her to. In the C living area there was a unit with a great deal of personal independence. Though the staff felt that this unit might be too unstructured for Bev, it was decided to try her there on a daycare program. She would remain on Unit VIII as her residence, but participate with the C unit for her daytime activities. After a few weeks of the daycare trial, it was decided that Bev could not be moved to C living area after all. Unfortunately, her behavior began to regress and she was becoming abusive again. The problem for Bev was that there was really no appropriate placement for her. Though she no longer needed the strict program of Unit VIII, she wasn't ready for the independence of the C units. Even though Bev had made tremendous progress, she still had issues that required special attention. She needed a middle ground that, unfortunately, didn't exist. Instead of transferring, she remained on Unit VIII and was given as much off ward time as possible. It was the best scenario the staff could arrange.

Before the move to another unit was tried, a great deal of thought had gone into Bev's possible transfer. Many meetings were held with psychologists, caseworkers, doctors, nurses, and other staff trying to determine the best course of action. Psychological evaluations were also done as part of the decision making process. An evaluation done in April of 1974 says that Bev had made significant improvements in her behavior and social interaction since moving to Unit VIII. It gives all sorts of test results, but, as usual, also says that Bev does not perform well in a testing situation. She becomes unresponsive and inattentive, talks in a whisper, and gives many bizarre answers to questions. This was par for the course for Bev. Since childhood, every time she was put in a testing situation, she stressed and refused to perform to the best of her ability. This habit had tragic results for her. This evaluation report explains why:

> The tests administered before and just after admission indicate that Beverly was functioning in the moderate range...In her early years it is mentioned that she could probably have done more if she had not been so uncooperative... During most of Beverly's 22 years at Pennhurst she was so uncontrollable that she was not permitted to participate in any training program.

These statements underline the unfortunate course of Bev's life at Pennhurst. Bev was a child who had come to Pennhurst with potential that was never realized because she was undone by her lack of self control. When in the public school she couldn't succeed in their conventional program, she was taken out with no alternative placement available. The same thing happened at Pennhurst. When she didn't fit into the classroom structure, there was no alternative. As a result, Bev had never been given a chance to learn much of anything during her childhood and adolescence. She was left to languish and regress when, with proper management and instruction, she very likely could have bloomed into a fairly high functioning adult.

So 22 years later, here was Bev with the chance to reclaim some of that lost potential. It was late in the game, but there was still a chance. Though she never made the transfer to a less restrictive unit, she continued to make good progress in Unit VIII. Her annual program review a year later in 1975 paints a picture of a person making great strides. She continued to learn new personal care skills, attended occupational therapy and music therapy, and started to learn tasks in the workshop. Despite all her progress, she still had her violent outbursts and still needed to be restrained on occasion, although this was happening less frequently. The report says that Bev was functioning higher than most of the other residents in Unit VIII, but that the noise and confusion on the ward upset her and triggered some of her abusive behavior. There was a continuing problem of no appropriate placing for Bev. She should have been on a open ward, but no open wards with the high staff to resident ratio that Bev required existed at that time. She remained caught in a kind of limbo, which slowed her progress toward independence.

Bev had always needed a lot of attention from staff, which she was not able to get in the C units. The biggest advantage to remaining in Q Building Unit VIII was the staff-to-resident ratio, which was usually one to three. Before she moved there, Bev had lived on wards where the ratio was one to 25 or more, making it impossible for staff to give her individual attention. Only on Unit VIII would there be enough trained staff to help residents like Bev meet their extreme challenges. One of the skills Bev struggled with the most was socialization. She usually preferred sitting alone rather than interacting with her peers. Her closest relationships were with staff, and there was one mental retardation aide in particular that she became especially attached to. Though she could carry on a limited conversation with someone when prompted, she rarely initiated conversation on her own. She would rather sit alone with her own thoughts than talk with other people. There is no mention on her ever forming a real friendship with any of her fellow residents. Sometimes I think Bev might have avoided social contact to prevent getting in trouble. She was particularly sensitive to teasing, and it seems that other residents enjoyed teasing her, especially about her family. Bev often responded to such taunts with violence. This, in turn, often got her placed in isolation. After a while, isolation became a way of life for her, and she created it even when she was surrounded by people. She also is very noise sensitive and could become agitated when the ward became too loud. Tuning out became a way to cope with the chaos. Even today she is content to sit quietly in her own world during family get togethers while activity swirls around her. She is willing to participate briefly, but eventually we know she might want to retreat into a quiet corner and be still.

After the failed transfer, Bev stayed on in Unit VIII where she continued to bloom and gain more independence. In October of 1976, a very thorough annual program review describes an active life full of new experiences. Though her behavior continued to improve each year, she was kept on maintenance levels of antipsychotic drugs, along with medications needed to address the side effects of the powerful psychotropics. Bev would continue to need similar drugs for her entire life. These drugs helped keep head banging and hair pulling to a minimum and eliminated the need for restraints. Just as important, they helped her to be a happier person, less tormented by violent urges. In this report she is described as "very cooperative and friendly to all around her."

Although it was determined that Bev still needed the structure of Unit VIII, giving Bev learning experiences outside the Unit was a priority. Perhaps her favorite activity was swimming lessons. There was swimming instruction on campus, but Bev's participation during the summer when they used the outdoor pool was limited because she took Thorazine, which creates hypersensitivity to sunlight. Late in 1976, however, she began a group swimming program at nearby West Chester College where they used an indoor pool. Even though she was overweight, Bev liked all sorts of physical activities and took part in physical education classes, where she did very well. She also attended Pre-vocational Occupational Therapy which helped prepare her for work in a sheltered workshop. It taught her how to earn money and also how to spend it. This is where she developed her obsessive fondness for vending machines and a lifelong love affair with quarters. The organized activity she loved above all others was music therapy. Bev always enjoyed singing and dancing, and she was able to memorize the lyrics to dozens of songs. To this day listening to music, especially the golden oldies, will get Bev singing along and dancing. Though she was never able to learn to read, Bev loved books. Since I am a librarian, I was especially pleased to discover that she also went to the library and learned how to select books and listen to stories. The librarian even complimented her library skills! Not only did Bev take part in all of these activities, but she went to them by traveling around the Pennhurst campus independently, either walking from building to building or by riding on a bus. This is a woman who used to sit rocking back and forth in a day room for hours at a time. Now she was free to go almost anywhere on campus all on her own. It was truly a miraculous transformation.

In March of 1979, at the age of 35, Bev finally left Unit VIII. She was deemed ready to move into the Independence Unit, a home-like modular residence that prepared clients to live outside the institution they had known for so long. It had been a long journey for Bev to the Independence Unit, a journey that had taken almost ten years. Independence Unit was just one step away from the outside world and the closest thing to a normal life that she could experience at Pennhurst. The bedrooms there were much like college dorm rooms. The beds were covered with pretty spreads, pillows, and stuffed animals, and there was storage for personal items. The common areas were comfortable and inviting. Meals were served family style at dining tables. Residents gathered in pleasant recreation areas to watch TV and socialize. This last stop for patients before going out into a group home was meant to help them learn how to live in a way none of them had experienced since coming to Pennhurst. After years of merely being housed, they were actually going to live in a house.

At the time of this important event for Bev, the caseworkers at Pennhurst kept in close contact with Mother and Dad through both letters and phone calls. Records show that Dad even attended some meetings at Pennhurst. Unfortunately, during this period Mother faced some serious health problems. In the late 1970's, she was diagnosed with breast cancer, chose to have a lumpectomy, and followed that up with radiation treatments. Apparently she didn't inform the Pennhurst staff about what was going on. Notes in their records commented on the fact that Mother was not responding to their attempts to talk with her, and they were puzzled at her lack of response. This isn't surprising to me, since she did not share information about her cancer with her coworkers or friends, and gave even her family only the bits and pieces she absolutely had to reveal. Luckily, Dad stepped in and took an active part in Bev's transfer to the Independence Unit and continued to visit her from time to time. Even so, Mother kept Bev in her thoughts and sent her cards to stay in touch until she could see her again.

Bev seemed to handle the transition to Independence Modular 5 very well and, for a couple of years, she continued to thrive. Early in 1981, however, she began to have problems. Her behavior began to deteriorate as she reverted to some earlier habits like urinary accidents, banging her head, and swallowing inedible objects. She was in the infirmary off and on and finally went to the hospital for surgery on her prolapsed rectum, which had first caused her trouble over ten years earlier. It seems that the doctors were trying to find physical reasons for her deterioration. For some reason Bev's behavior could just not be stabilized, even though her medication was increased and she was in an intense behavior-shaping program. Though her actions were serious, and even at one point called "life threatening", one of her more amusing transgressions was stealing cookies out of the office in the workshop. Whether it was punching someone or stealing cookies, her maladaptive behaviors needed to be reshaped. Because she needed constant monitoring, after October 1982 she stayed in the program at Audubon Hall and never returned to Independence 5. She remained in Audubon until she left Pennhurst for good just over a year later.

From the moment Bev moved into Independence Unit, her social workers had begun trying to find her a community living arrangement. Coming up with an appropriate placement, however, was no easy task. Every spring, from 1979 to 1982, a letter came from the Berks County Office of Mental Health and Mental Retardation to the social worker assigned to Bev's case telling her that no CLA was currently available for her. However, in the spring of 1983, something different began to happen. Copies of Bev's Pennhurst records were systematically being sent to the Berks County MH/MR Office. As the records continued to be shared, letters discussing Bev's case also went back and forth between Pennhurst and the county MH/MR Office for several months. Finally, on December 13, 1983, a letter came to Pennhurst from an organization called Threshold Rehabilitation Services informing Bev that she would be moving to a Community Living Arrangement in her home town of Reading, PA and attending a day program at BERCO Industries: "We are pleased to inform you that you will be starting in our Residential CLA Program (Community Living Arrangement) on Thursday, December 15, 1983 at 10:30 AM."

Opening the Door

That simple typewritten sentence changed her life forever. She had a place to live, she had a job, she had her ticket to freedom. She was out!

BOOK THREE

1983 - 2015

Out!

Dear Ms. Miller:

I am pleased to inform you of your discharge from the Pennhurst Center effective September 26, 1984.

We wish you the very best in the future.

Sincerely yours,

George A. Kopchick, Jr.
Director

~14~

Don't Look Back

On September 27, 1984 Bev received two type written sentences from George A. Kopchick Jr., Director of the Pennhurst Center, informing her of her official discharge. That was how 32 years of life at Pennhurst ended. She was 41 years old. This brief letter, as dramatic as it is, was only a formality. Her new life had actually already begun nine months earlier when she took up residence in her Community Living Arrangement in Reading. On December 15, 1983, she had gotten into a car to be driven away from the grounds of the Pennhurst Center for the last time. She had no sense of the meaning of that moment. I'm sure she was happy to be going out and away on an adventure, but she had no idea what a grand adventure it was going to be.

When Bev left the campus of Pennhurst Center on that day, she never returned, but the opportunity to stay in her new group home was not guaranteed. Even though Judge Broderick's decision in the Halderman v. Pennhurst State School lawsuit mandated the relocation of all Pennhurst residents, the proper placement needed to be found for each individual. There were many factors that came into play once Bev left the institutional setting, and she was on a period of probation to see if her transition would be successful. That's why, even though she was placed in a group home, she wasn't taken off Pennhurst's rolls until nine months later. The social workers had to decide whether or not she was going to make it in the outside world. She was, after all, severely cognitively disabled, had been institutionalized for 32 years, and had a long list of maladaptive behaviors. It wasn't going to be easy.

After the court's decision, it took years to find enough community placements for all the residents of Pennhurst who needed to be moved, but Bev's turn finally came. An organization called Threshold worked with the Mental Health and Mental Retardation Office of Berks County to provide and administer the group home where Bev would reside. Her placement was in the city of Reading, Pennsylvania, only minutes away from where she was born. The house was a brick ranch located near a shopping mall where stores and restaurants were available to the residents. She had a female housemate, but each of them had her own bedroom. There was full time staff to take care of them and to shape the new behaviors that they would need in their more independent life. Before Bev made the move into her new home, there was a long structured transition period. The team that would be responsible for her welfare first started visiting her at Pennhurst so that she could get to know them. The next step in the process was taking her to the house for some overnight stays so that she could become familiar with her new surroundings. Only after she seemed comfortable with both the staff and the house did she actually move in.

During this transitional period parental involvement was highly encouraged by the team. In the beginning, Mother and Dad attended meetings together to discuss Bev's move so that they both could take part in the planning phase. Staff and social workers urged them to take a more active role in Bev's life. Yet, though they were both thrilled with the prospect of having their daughter leave Pennhurst to lead a more normal life, neither one of them changed their longstanding distant relationship with her. With the group home less than a half hour away from each of them, visiting would have been so much easier and they could have spent more time with her. Instead, they both maintained the same visitation schedule they always had, seeing Bev primarily on holidays and birthdays. Mother, of course, was hampered by the fact that she couldn't drive. Though Dad did stop in at the group home occasionally, he arranged very few scheduled visits. Though they now were more informed about Bev's health and welfare on a regular basis and attended annual plan of care meetings, they still remained passive participants in her life. The details of her daily life were left to the Threshold staff. After having given up most of their parental rights many years ago, it was hard for them to figure out how to be Bev's mom and dad again.

In her new home, one of the first things Bev had to learn how to do was to live cooperatively with a housemate. Bev had never really learned to form friendships and had always preferred interacting with staff to being with her peers, much as she had always preferred interacting with her parents at home rather than with her brother and sisters. It was going to take a long time for her to develop any real interest in her housemates. Not just for Bev, but for all the residents in the program, finding the right mix of housemates was extremely important and took some experimentation. Compatibility was only one factor. Even when they got along well, it took time to form true relationships.

One of the biggest obstacles to Bev's chance for success in the outside world was her array of maladaptive behaviors. Even after years of behavior modification efforts at Pennhurst, Bev still hung onto many unacceptable, even dangerous, actions. When she was frustrated she still wanted to pull her hair out and bang her head against walls or floors. She could still lose her temper and strike out at the people around her. Her bathroom habits were unreliable. She loved to stuff toilet paper into the toilets and sometimes dunked her head in the toilet bowl. At times she forgot about the bathroom altogether and soiled herself. She also had a habit of putting inedible objects in her mouth and occasionally even ate the nuts and bolts she handled in the workshop. Even though these behaviors began to fade after she left Pennhurst, she still needed constant monitoring and behavior-shaping techniques to keep them under control. Of course, she absolutely had to have the proper medications every day in order to be able to function both at home and in her workplace. As long as Bev is properly medicated she is peaceful and cooperative, and her daily medication cocktail has been adjusted many times through the years.

Despite all of these challenges, Bev began to adapt to her new life quite well. In order to help her through this period of adjustment, she had what was called a Temporary Individual Habilitation Plan. This was a behavioral management plan developed by a team of caseworkers, psychologists, and other mental health specialists from both Pennhurst and Threshold. Two meetings were held to discuss this plan, one before Bev left Pennhurst and one shortly after she began living in her group home.

Both Mother and Dad attended both of these meetings and signed the necessary permission forms. When Bev made the move to her new home, a behavioral specialist was assigned to the residence to oversee the implementation of the plan. Luckily, Bev responded well and continued to adjust to her new life with fewer and fewer episodes of agitation or compulsive actions. In June, after a six month period, she was reevaluated and a recommendation was made for her official discharge from Pennhurst. By September the paperwork was completed, and she received her formal notice.

Not everyone who left the institution for community group homes had the same experience, but for Bev getting out of the Pennhurst environment was the best thing that could have happened to her. To have a peaceful place to live that was free of the noise and chaotic energy of the institution, to have her time filled with meaningful activity in the sheltered workshop, to have a reassuring daily routine in familiar surroundings, and to have a caring team of people devoting their attention to her as an individual helped her grow into a new person. Each day outside the walls of Pennhurst was a step toward a completely new life. She began to bloom. And she began to smile.

Bev's first group home in Reading was just one of several that she would reside in over the years, run by an organization called Threshold Rehabilitation Services. This non-profit organization was established in 1965 to provide transitional support for people who were leaving state centers to live in community settings. Since then they have continued to provide a variety of services to people like Bev with mental, emotional, physical and developmental challenges. At the time that Bev left Pennhurst, there were few group homes in existence in Pennsylvania. The concept of community living arrangements for the mentally disabled was still in its infancy. It wasn't until the large institutions began to close that small group homes and apartments became a viable alternative for the people who once resided there. Organizations like Threshold needed to find suitable houses to buy or rent. Not just any house would do. They preferred homes with one story so that they could easily be made handicapped accessible. They looked for neighborhoods close to shopping, doctors, and public transportation. After they located appropriate houses, they hired and trained staff to provide the necessary care and services that their consumers needed. The people they served had a variety of mental and physical disabilities and needed a wide spectrum of programs offered by both government and private organizations. At first most of these services were coordinated by the Berks County Mental Health/Mental Retardation Office, but in 1987 they formed the Service Access Management to act as case managers. In 1997 this organization became a private non-profit human services company that continues to expand its outreach today. Just as these organizations were pioneers in the field of independence for people with mental disabilities, Pennhurst residents like Bev were pioneers. As members of the class action suit against the Commonwealth of Pennsylvania, they blazed a trail through new territory and showed the way for thousands of others who would someday follow their lead. They were part of a grand experiment that would forever change the way mentally challenged people would be educated, employed, and integrated into their communities.

When Bev began living in her group homes, she also started working at a paying job. The organization responsible for that opportunity is called Prospectus BERCO. This non-profit group was founded in 1977 to provide services to people with disabilities and the elderly in Berks County. Their day program includes supervised workshops where people do assembly line jobs like folding boxes, putting products into blister packages, or applying labels to bags and cartons. These workshops are safe and friendly places for mentally and physically disabled people to work and earn a paycheck. Bev worked there for almost twenty years and was one of their best workers. Besides having very good manual dexterity, she could learn and perform tasks that had multiple steps to complete. She did such an outstanding job that she received several achievement awards. Bev really likes to be busy and thought being on the production line at BERCO was great fun, although her favorite part of the day was undoubtedly break time, when she could take her beloved quarters to the vending machines and get sodas and snacks. Even though she retired over ten years ago, she still talks excitedly about getting soda at break time, and to this day she can't pass a vending machine without going over to check the return slot for any loose change carelessly left behind.

Since Bev left Pennhurst she has lived in five different group homes, although group homes were only one type of community living arrangement available for the former Pennhurst residents. Higher functioning individuals could live on their own or with roommates in apartments. That wasn't an option for Bev, but another choice for her was called a Family Living Program. This type of arrangement provided another alternative to group homes. Instead of residing in a house under the care of paid staff, a Threshold consumer would move into a home where she was treated as an actual member of the family. In August of 1991 Bev left her group home to enter into a Family Living Program. The people who were fostering Bev were supposed to incorporate her into their daily routines and provide her with a more normal family life. There are no records available to me to explain what happened, but the arrangement apparently didn't work out very well.

It doesn't surprise me that Bev didn't do well in the Family Living Program. Bev craved a family, but the one she went to live with was not able to fulfill her needs. She had her own ideas about what a family should be. Bev missed her real mother and wanted her, not a substitute. Unfortunately Mother was having serious health problems at that time and hadn't been able to see Bev for many months. Her cancer, which had been in remission for a decade, had returned and began spreading with a vengeance. As the cancer progressed through her body, dementia was taking hold of her mind. By the spring of 1991, unable to manage on her own anymore, she began residing in an assisted living center. To make matters worse, during this time when Mother was unable to see Bev, Dad also curtailed his time with her by spending six months of the year in Florida. Missing her family had always made Bev anxious and agitated. That, along with the changes in her living arrangements, was too much for her to handle. In addition, the increased amount of independence she had in her new home would only make the situation worse for her. After 32 years of institutionalization, and with a mental age of about six, she could not flourish in an environment where she was expected to make her own decisions and act independently. Instead of feeling free, she felt lost.

Bev still craves a lot of emotional support and needs a great deal of structure in her daily routine. The group home setting with trained staff gives her just the right amount of independence and guidance to help her, and that is where she can thrive and be the happiest. As it turned out, the Family Living Program was not the right situation for Bev. After trying the FLP for about a year, Bev was back in yet another group home where she suffered a psychiatric emergency that required hospitalization. As a result of her emotional crisis, she was put under the care of a psychiatrist who prescribed three different psychotropic drugs to help keep her calm and balanced. Ever since then, she has been monitored on a regular basis by a psychiatrist and her medications are carefully adjusted as needed.

Although her life outside the walls of Pennhurst was dramatically better and happier for her, it still was not without its difficulties. There were many challenges to overcome, and there were times when Bev's maladaptive behaviors resurfaced and caused problems. In rare instances she became so unmanageable that she needed psychiatric hospitalization. This has happened several times during her years in group homes. Bev doesn't tolerate change very well, and any changes in residence, staff, or roommates could upset her. Inevitably, for a variety of reasons, changes have been necessary during the twenty eight years that she has been in community living arrangements. Housemates come and go, staff turnover is common, and housing reassignments sometimes occur. Health problems and medication adjustments can also cause a lot of stress. Bev does remarkably well most of the time, but occasionally the stress becomes overwhelming and she has a meltdown. That is what happened with the Family Living Program, and medical intervention was necessary.

Once she was stabilized in the hospital, she was placed in yet another group home where she would remain for the next four years. That home was a rambling house outside a small town not far from Reading. Not long after Bev moved there late in 1992, her mother passed away. It was almost as if with each move Bev made, she left her mother further and further behind until their separation finally became complete after her death. After she lost her mother, she felt bewildered by her disappearance. Even though the house she was living in at the time was a bright, comfortable place in a lovely country setting, Bev never really seemed happy there. It was a large house with several bedrooms and a variety of common spaces including a bowling alley in the basement! Surrounding the house were beautiful grounds where the residents could enjoy being outdoors. That advantage was lost on Bev who never really enjoyed being outdoors very much and has always preferred being inside. Besides that, because her psychotropic drugs make her sensitive to sunlight, she never could spend a lot of time outside. Jonnie and I occasionally visited her at that house both with Dad and on our own.

Though we were impressed with the accommodations, we weren't sure that Bev really felt at home there. Eventually that facility was closed and Bev made one last move in the summer of 1996. Eerily, just after she moved to her new group home, her father passed away. Now she was an orphan.

Her new home on the outskirts of Reading is where she still lives in today. It is a comfortable ranch house in a pleasant residential area adjacent to a large public school complex. By coincidence, the high school just down the street is the one her brother Greg graduated from in 1960. She shares the home with two housemates, currently both males following the death of a female resident who lived to be 100 years old. Bev has her own bright bedroom with an en suite bathroom. Her closet is

crammed with pretty clothes and the top of her dresser is covered with family photographs and personal mementos. Since Bev has a history of bronchitis and pneumonia, she sleeps in a bed which elevates her at night to aid in her breathing, and she has equipment nearby to supply oxygen when she needs it. In the basement of the house there is exercise equipment for her to work out on to help with weight control and overall fitness. Recently a stair lift has been installed to help the residents get up and down from the basement and garage area more easily. The rest of the house consists of a living room with a large screen TV, an open dining area and a kitchen. It is a cozy little house that is warm and inviting. Threshold makes sure the home is run according to strict guidelines, and a staff person is with the residents twenty four hours a day to make their lives as comfortable and secure as possible.

Through the years Bev and her two housemates have become their own little family. The staff have come to love them like their own family and they gladly go the extra mile to do all they can for them. They have a good life. It has been a long road for Bev from Pennhurst to where she is now, and it has taken a lot of dedicated people to help her get there. It wasn't easy, but against all odds she made it. And even though she may not realize it, she is home.

~15~

In Loco Parentis

After Pennhurst, Greg, Jonnie, and I had very little to do with Bev's new life other than the occasional get together with her either at Mother's apartment or Dad's bungalow. Bev remained a distant figure in the background of our daily affairs. Our parents rarely discussed anything to do with her care, legal status, health, or their post-divorce visitations policy, and we rarely asked. After our parents' death, however, everything changed. Suddenly, there she was. It was only then that she became a real person to me. Finally, after forty nine years, I uncovered my eyes to really look at my older sister, to really see her. It was as if an artist, who had drawn a rough sketch of a person, began to fill in the details, the contours and colors that would eventually lead to a finished portrait.

I began to realize that so much of my relationship with Bev was based on the past. I had never stopped thinking of her as the little girl who threw temper tantrums and was sent away to learn how to behave. The person who resided at Pennhurst had ceased to be my sister and became a stranger so distant and damaged that I felt that we no longer had any connection. I knew it was time to learn how to relate to the Beverley that had emerged into adulthood and was living her own full and happy life. It was an epiphany, and it opened doors to places in my heart that had been closed for many years. It also created a newfound curiosity that led me to learn more about Bev, and more about myself and our family in the process.

The loss of our parents affected all of us deeply, of course, but for Bev, in particular, it was devastating. It took me years to realize what Bev really lost when her parents died. It changed her life in a way the rest of us could never imagine. Her parents were her world, her only connection to the old self vaguely remembered in the shadows of her mind where lives the little girl who curled up on her daddy's lap to be hugged and tickled, who sat in the shady backyard drinking lemonade and eating fresh baked cookies, who spent contented days with her mother, singing and learning her letters and numbers and listening to story books. When her parents went away those happy memories lost their anchor.

Mother passed away in 1993, Dad in 1996. In both cases their loss was more a fading away than an abrupt change for Bev. Because of their illnesses, both of them had been seeing her less and less for months, even years, before their actual passing. Both of them died of cancer, and both of them went into slow and painful declines during which they did not see Bev at all. I truly can't remember when either of them saw her for the last time. Bev was left to wonder where they were, and none of us siblings thought to take her feelings into consideration during all that time. Her parents had somehow disappeared. They never came to see her anymore. They had gone with no goodbyes.

When they passed away we all assumed that Bev wouldn't understand the concept of death. We didn't want to upset her by coming right out and saying they were dead. We certainly didn't want to tell her she would never see them again. We used euphemisms, saying they went to heaven and she would see them there. We assured her that we would all take care of her until she could be with her parents in heaven. We gave her lots of family photographs to display in her bedroom. I don't know if they give her any comfort or make her happy when she looks at them. I do know that her mom and dad are very much alive in her mind, and I think she would not be one bit surprised to have either of them walk in the door one day and give her a hug.

Our mother's health began to decline in the late 1970's when she discovered a lump in her breast and was diagnosed with cancer. She referred to it coyly as her "lumpy." At that time she was in her late fifties and still working full-time on the production line at the local Western Electric plant. True to form she was very circumspect about her condition. She kept it a secret from her coworkers and shared very little information with anyone, even with her children. Without discussing it with her family, she elected to have a lumpectomy, but didn't reveal details of the surgery until it was over. Afterward she underwent radiation treatments, but no chemotherapy, and began taking a drug called tamoxifen, which was used to help prevent the breast cancer from recurring. When we asked her about the whole process, she acted as though it were no more difficult than getting a tooth pulled. No fuss, no muss, no bother. That was her way. Luckily, her course of treatment was very successful. She had few side effects and missed very little work time, not even enough to arouse suspicion among her coworkers. She kept her illness completely secret from everyone except her family and her two closest friends, and went on with her life as if nothing had happened.

In 1984, the same year Bev left Pennhurst, Mother retired from her job and began to live a quiet life in her apartment near center city Reading. Her apartment was the first floor of an old row house in a tree shaded neighborhood with easy access to downtown. Her oddball landlords, a childless married couple in their golden years, lived on the upper floors of the house and kept an eye out for her welfare, popping in to see her more often than she would have liked. Her years of travel and dating and socializing were over by then. She developed a comfortable routine in her life, which now centered around her family and a very few special friends. Other than weekly forays into the town center to do errands and shopping, Mother stayed at home and let the world come to her. She became a sort of family matriarch who never forgot a birthday or anniversary, and who still liked to celebrate holidays with the simple traditions we had followed for years. Our family was closer than it had been for a long time, and Bev was part of it again.

Jonnie and her husband and children, my husband and I, and Bev all gathered at Mother's apartment to be together on holidays and birthdays. The staff at the group home brought Bev to these occasions and picked her up again at the end of the day. Bev loved these times and felt secure in the predictability of each visit. She started the day alone with her mom, having some quality bonding time. Then the rest of us descended on the place, and the excitement began. Lots of food, gifts, and happy commotion. Then off she went back to her group home, babbling all the while about coming back again for her next special day. These were happy times for her, but they were not to last.

Everything was rosy until Mother's health took a turn for the worse. After almost ten good years while her cancer was in remission, her luck ran out and she went into a slow but steady decline. Though the cancer was eventually to return, it was a mental decline that happened first. By the late 1980's, Mother had become clinically depressed and dementia slowly began to creep in. Our grandmother had developed dementia as well, though at a later age, so it wasn't surprising to see it appearing in Mother. The first signs were subtle. She no longer went into town to socialize with her Penn Street buddies at the local shops, she stopped doing crossword puzzles and reading, she kept the apartment's windows closed and locked without air conditioning on the hottest summer days. It appeared that financial worries were at the root of her depressed state. After her retirement, she was obsessed with the idea of being able to leave us money when she passed away and dreamed of hitting it big in the lottery in order to make that dream come true. She spent hundreds, probably thousands, of dollars on lottery tickets. She won small amounts of cash, but never the big score. When she realized that her time was running out and she was never going to win a big jackpot, she lost all hope and became depressed. Anti-depressant medication helped for a while, and she bounced back for a short time. But truth came knocking at her door and there was no hiding from it. She had always known that one day her cancer would return, and now the doctors were beginning to see signs that the time had come.

By 1990 her cancer had returned with a vengeance and was spreading rapidly throughout her body - lungs, bone marrow, and liver. This time the doctors recommended chemotherapy and, since she needed to rely on Jonnie to transport her back and forth from her treatments, she had to reveal the truth to us. As her chemotherapy progressed, Mother's mental health began to decline even further, and once the antidepressant drugs stopped working, dementia took control. She locked herself in her apartment in a state of paranoia, afraid of everything and everyone. She lost track of time, stopped making meals, and became unable to make even the smallest decisions. She telephoned both Jonnie and me severaltimes a day and forgot she had ever talked to us as soon as she hung up the phone. When I got an answering machine to screen her calls, she would talk to the machine as if I were actually on the other end of the line. Once anxiety and depression began to overwhelm her, Mother no longer felt able to manage Bev's visits, and later, when the chemotherapy began, she was too weak and debilitated even to take care of herself. She called the staff at the group home and told them not to bring Bev to see her anymore. Bev gradually faded into some sort of limbo of lost memory, out of sight, out of mind.

By this time Mother was alone. She had never remarried and had no husband to care for her in her old age. The younger man who had helped her to engineer her divorce was no longer part of her life. After the divorce, they continued their relationship for several years and were very happy together, but they never married. I'm sure they discussed marriage, but in the end decided against it. He was much younger and was certainly looking for a new mom for his two little boys, while our mother already had grandchildren. They were both also well aware that Jonnie and I didn't like him. It was not a promising situation. True to form, Mother never discussed their relationship with us, especially since she was aware of our disapproval. I have no idea exactly when he stepped out of her life. Afterwards, Mother dated occasionally, but she never found anyone to share her life again and wound up without a partner at the end of her life. Our father loved her deeply and would have come back to her in a flash, but she would have none of it. He offered help many times, but she was too proud to accept. Nevertheless, he held out hope to the very end, and he was in love with her until the day she died.

Even though either Jonnie or I drove down every week to do errands for her, to take her shopping, and to stock up on food which she rarely ate, she told her friends we never came to see her. One day I answered a knock at the apartment door to find one of her friends standing there with a casserole in her hands, convinced that she needed to keep our mother from starving because we were neglecting her. This particular woman actually fostered Mother's dementia-fueled paranoia to the point that she threatened to report us to social services. It was at that point that Jonnie finally said enough was enough. She contacted Mother's primary physician, who referred us to a nearby assisted living facility. Before she had time to protest, we packed her suitcases, drove her to the facility, and convinced her to sign the papers. Although at first we were wracked with guilt, we knew it was for the best. In the weeks that followed we cleaned out her apartment and furnished her new residence with her favorite possessions. She now had a cozy, comfortable suite where she was safe and had all of her needs taken care of. We all could finally breathe a sigh of relief.

The move from apartment to assisted living was completed in the spring of 1991. Although she had not wanted to go, once she was there, she was quite contented. Because she felt safe there, her anxiety level went way down and both her mental and physical health improved. The staff made sure she took her medications on schedule, she ate regular healthy meals in the communal dining room, she took part in group activities and had lots of new acquaintances to talk with. As a result, the progress of her dementia slowed dramatically. She was doing so well that, when the doctors suggested another round of chemotherapy, we decided not to do it. We wanted her to have a good quality of life in the short time she had left. However, even though she was thriving in her new residence, she was still dealing with the ravages of dementia. Eventually she fell into a state of mind in which she could comprehend only what was going on at the moment. The past was hazy, the future non-existent. The matriarch who had always kept in contact with her family through cards and notes and telephone calls simply sat and waited for cards and calls to come to her. She acknowledged them briefly, then soon forgot them, even though we displayed the cards and photographs on her dresser where she could see them constantly. Luckily, she kept a positive attitude as she lapsed into a kind of fuzzy contentment.

For over a year Mother did quite well at the assisted living center until a new problem emerged. Even before she went to live there, Mother had been having difficulty walking. She moved very slowly and often lost her balance. In the sheltered environment of the facility, with hand railings and elevators, she got around well enough, but there was a regulation that all residents needed to be able to evacuate the building in the event of fire. As time went on, Mother was no longer able to get out in an acceptable amount of time during the fire drills. The staff was discussing moving her room closer to an exit when fate stepped in to solve the dilemma. One night in September of 1992, as Mother was getting out of bed, she fell and broke her collar bone. She was admitted to the hospital and spent two weeks there while doctors tried to figure out why she was losing her balance.

In Loco Parentis

While she was a patient in the hospital she turned 70 years old. We celebrated her special day in her hospital room with a cake and gifts and grandchildren by her bedside. We were very surprised when, in the midst of the festivities, she told us that Dad had stopped by for a visit as well. Through the years we knew that he had popped in occasionally to see her wherever she was - without her permission, of course. Though she showed her usual consternation when she told us about it, I think she was secretly glad to see him and pleased that he had remembered her birthday. As it turned out, it was the last time they ever saw each other.

The tests she had in the hospital were never conclusive, but during her stay she was given physical therapy and then referred for further physical rehabilitation. We moved Mother to a rehabilitation center near my home, where she spent a few weeks, but made little progress. Walking became increasingly more difficult, and it was obvious that she was getting weaker instead of stronger. We found a personal care facility that would give her a few more weeks of relative independence, a place all on one floor where she could get around in a wheelchair. When we visited her there at Christmas, however, we realized that her health was rapidly failing. She was listless, dehydrated, and mentally confused. Just after New Year's Day in 1993, Jonnie took her to the emergency room of the local hospital, where doctors advised her to check Mother into a nursing home. She went by ambulance right from the hospital to a nursing home not far from Jonnie's house. With good nursing care, she perked up a bit, and we were encouraged by the improvement. Unfortunately, after only five weeks, she developed pneumonia, went into a coma, and passed away very quickly. We were all in shock, unprepared for the sudden loss. As usual, she made no fuss about leaving and did it in the same quiet, resolute way that she had lived her life.

After Mother went into the assisted living center, she never mentioned Bev. She didn't ask to see her, and, for some reason, we never took it upon ourselves to bring her to see Mother at the facility. Because by the time Mother began residing there, her walking had become very slow and unsteady, she rarely went out. For a while she was still able come for visits with us at home, but not for long. Soon visits to Jonnie's house were no longer possible because her family lived on the second floor above her husband's workshop and the steps were too steep for Mother to negotiate. Fortunately, since there were no physical barriers

145

at my home, she was able to come there more often. Her very last time away from a residential care facility was Thanksgiving Day in 1992, when she had a quiet holiday dinner with me and my husband at our house less than three months before she died. For the most part though, since it was a long drive to either of our homes, it was so much easier for everyone to go to her than for her to come to us. After a while Bev was no longer included in our arrangements, and holidays and birthdays came and went without her. Jonnie and I were so busy trying to take care of Mother that we had forgotten about Bev.) *yes !*

Once Mother went into the nursing home, we knew her days were numbered. We called our brother in Brazil, and he flew back to the States to be with us and help to prepare for the inevitable end. Still, we never thought of bringing Bev to the nursing home so that she and Mother could see each other one last time. Though Mother's mind was slipping away, she was lucid enough that I think she would have known Bev if she saw her. I felt helpless in dealing with Mother's impending death and was in the process of contacting hospice to guide us through her final days. Perhaps then we would have arranged for Bev to come for a visit. Unfortunately, events progressed too quickly and we never got the chance to get preparations underway. Pneumonia took her too fast. She died on February 12, 1993. She had not seen her daughter Beverley for well over two years.

Luckily for Bev, during those two years when her mother was unable to see her anymore, her father stepped in and made sure she had extra visits at his home. Bev loved visiting with her dad. He lived in a little rustic bungalow by a creek outside a small country village. There she was able to spend time outdoors, which is something she didn't get to do very often. Jonnie and I, and even Greg when he was in the States, visited there with Dad and Bev and spent many happy afternoons together. Greg came with his wife Chris, I came with my husband Greg, Jonnie usually brought her two young daughters and, occasionally, her husband Dave. We would spend a Sunday afternoon there, nothing formal, just hanging out and enjoying some family time. Sometimes we had lunch, or cake and ice cream, and sat outside in lawn chairs and savored the summer weather. Dad was a free spirit, always joking around and making Bev laugh. He let her eat whatever she wanted and spoiled her with lots of candy and other sweets. In the summertime, life was good. The winters were another story.

Around the same time that Mother went into assisted living, our father bought a small house in Florida and began spending his winters there. That meant that for six months out of the year, including the major holidays that meant so much to her, Bev had no "home" to go to. Dad left for Florida each November and didn't return until May. When he came north for the summer months, he did spend time with Bev, but for six long months she saw neither of her parents. As a matter of fact, she had no family contact with any of us. We had gotten into the habit of leaving Bev's welfare up to our parents. Before they passed away we never thought about having Bev come to either Jonnie's or my house for visits, and though Greg was living in Brazil, when he did come home on furlough, he did not make seeing Bev a priority. The truth is that none of us really felt comfortable being with her on our own. *yes*

Even though Bev still had her dad, she dearly missed her mother and no one was ever able to fill that void in her life. After our parents' divorce in 1965, though Dad had a series of girlfriends, only one of them ever really got involved with Bev. The mistress who broke up the marriage, and with whom Dad had the longest relationship, did spend some time with Bev. Because she expected our father to marry her, she tried to become familiar with all of his children. Needless to say, none of us was terribly thrilled with the situation, but she was a nice woman and we liked her, despite the awkward fact that our mother hated her. We also were aware that our father would never marry her because he was still in love with Mother. Nevertheless, she was kind to Bev and supported Dad's parental efforts. Eventually she realized that Dad had no intention of marrying her and their relationship fizzled. The rest of Dad's many girlfriends were not people that Jonnie and I wanted anything to do with, and I doubt that any of them had any desire to spend time with any of us either, least of all Bev. So it went that when Dad had Bev for her visits at the bungalow, the girlfriends were not there, until he met Rose.

Dad started seeing Rose the year our mother passed away. Before Mother's death, our father held out hope that someday they would get back together, either in marriage, or at least in friendship. He never stopped loving her, and as long as she was alive, no other woman would ever be more than a temporary romantic interest. Although he had been unfaithful to her countless times, he loved her deeply and had never truly loved anyone else. When Rose came into his life, Mother was gone, and Dad finally decided to find someone to keep him company in his old age. It was an odd relationship. Rose was a former Roman Catholic nun who had left her order to enter the secular world. Though our dad was certainly no saint, they must have found some sort of common ground, because their courtship progressed rapidly, and in November of 1994 they were married.

Although after their marriage Rose was technically Bev's stepmother, that relationship was never established between them. In fact, none of us ever regarded her as a stepmother. We were all in our late forties or early fifties and not really in need of a new mother. I myself always referred to her as "my father's wife." Since Dad and Rose were married less than two years before his death, there was little time for us to get to know her, especially when they spent six months of each of those years in Florida. Bev certainly had no idea who Rose was other than a nice lady named "Rosie" who was with her dad when she visited at his house. Although Rose had good intentions, she never really knew how to relate to Bev. She was a former school principal and staunch Roman Catholic who expected Bev to respond to her with affection and gratitude. Though she very much wanted Bev to consider her a mother figure, even call her "Mom", Bev never did. Rose just couldn't accept the fact that Bev would always look upon her as just one of the many people who walked in and out of her life. Bev wanted her real mother and no one else would do.

The truth is that Dad's new wife Rose never had much of a chance to become part of our family. Again, fate was not kind. Dad and Rose had been married less than a year when he developed a malignant melanoma on his back. Because he was a Christian Scientist, he didn't seek medical treatment in the early stages of the disease. Instead, he prayed and contacted church practitioners to pray for him as well. By the time Rose finally convinced him to see a doctor about it, the melanoma was deeply entrenched and had spread to nearby lymph nodes. In desperation, despite his religious beliefs, Dad reluctantly consented to surgery. The melanoma was removed by a surgeon in Florida, but the results were not good. The tumor was so deep that skin grafts from Dad's thigh were necessary to close the wound, and it never healed properly. Shortly after the first surgery, Dad underwent another one to remove several lymph nodes under his arm. Still the cancer continued to spread. By the time he and Rose returned from Florida in the spring, Dad was in severe pain, weak and depressed.

In July we gave him a seventy fifth birthday party at a restaurant near his bungalow. He put on a brave face, but we could tell he was suffering. He was pale and shaky and had no appetite. To make matters worse, as Dad's health continued to fail, Rose was diagnosed with early breast cancer and had to undergo radiation treatments while she cared for her critically ill husband. Jonnie and I stepped in to help where we could, and all of us tried to spend time with Dad in his last few months. He was in and out of the hospital several times, but the doctors could do little for him. At the eleventh hour, Dad made a desperate decision to undergo chemotherapy. It was a useless effort that only made him sicker and weaker. He suffered through a miserable summer, languishing in his beloved little house by the creek, watching the birds on the feeders outside his window as his life ebbed away. On September 4, 1996, two days after he entered a hospice family respite center, he passed away.

Once both of her parents were gone, someone needed to step in to look after Bev's welfare. At first, Rose assumed that she would be the one to take over as a parent, but without Dad in the picture, Bev didn't recognize Rose as a mother figure. Rose had no experience at being a parent, and she certainly didn't know Bev very well after spending only sporadic visitation days with her. Although Rose felt that she should be the one to step in and oversee Bev's care, my sister Jonnie and I weren't so ready to relinquish critical decision making to her. We felt that we were better prepared to know what was best for Bev and became stubbornly protective of her. Besides, we also represented our mother's wishes, and that caused big problems. As Dad's second wife, Rose didn't appreciate our loyalty to our mother.

The first power struggle revolved around, of all things, burial arrangements. Long before our mother passed away, she went to a funeral home to arrange for not only her own funeral needs, but Bev's as well. She arranged for both herself and Bev to be cremated, though she made no arrangements for the disposition of the ashes. When our mother died she was cremated and her ashes buried with her parents and sisters in a Polish cemetery not far from where she grew up. She left it up to us to decide where Bev would be buried or scattered. We soon found out that Rose had other intentions.

As a Roman Catholic Rose believed in preservation of the body after death. She arranged for our father to be embalmed and buried intact. That was her decision to make, but she rankled us by disregarding our mother's wishes when it came to Bev's burial arrangements. Rose insisted that Bev not be cremated and that she be interred with herself and Dad on a cemetery plot our father had bought years before in a quaint old country churchyard near his bungalow. To further her plan, she ordered a huge gravestone and had it engraved with names and dates for Dad, herself, and Bev.

When Jonnie and I went to visit our father's grave we were appalled to see the stone, not only because of Rose's audacity, but because Beverley's birthdate was incorrect and her name was spelled without the "e" that only Mother ever remembered to use. It just seemed to reinforce the fact that Rose was not Bev's mother. A mother would never mistake the date when her child was born. A mother would never misspell her own child's name. The headstone sat there as a silent testament to a sad situation. To make matters even more ironic, several years after Dad's death, Rose returned to the Roman Catholic Church, and actually disavowed her marriage to our father. She no longer had any intention of ever being buried next to a man she claimed had never been her husband. She wanted nothing to do with any of us.

Immediately after Dad's death, however, Rose had tried to stay involved in Bev's life. Each year a meeting was held between Threshold and the families of the group home residents to discuss the plan of care for the coming year. From 1984 to 1995 Dad had attended Bev's meetings. When my father was ill with cancer in 1996, Jonnie and I went to the annual meeting with Rose to represent the family on his behalf. Right from the start it became clear that we and Rose did not see eye to eye on many issues concerning our sister, including the burial arrangements. Once again, Jonnie and I dug in and formed a battle line.

Our tenuous relationship with our stepmother cooled. Rose's feelings were hurt, and she turned her back on us. After we buried Dad in September of 1996, Rose wrapped up his affairs and prepared to leave for Florida, as usual, in November. As Dad's wife she had inherited everything he owned. He had two modest houses, his summer home in Pennsylvania and his winter home in Florida. He had few possessions, but what little he had, Rose kept for herself. None of us children received anything more than one wristwatch apiece as a remembrance of our father. Rose distanced herself from us both physically and emotionally. As a matter of fact, once she was in Florida, she decided to stay there. She returned North only to dispose of the little bungalow in Pennsylvania and make arrangements to move to Florida permanently. For a while we sent cards to her and made the occasional phone call, but eventually Rose cut off all contact with us. Once she had resumed her relationship with the Roman Catholic Church, her relationship with our family ceased. Though Greg still made an effort to stay in touch, Jonnie and I both eventually gave up trying.

For a couple of years after she moved to Florida, she did stay in contact with Bev through cards and telephone calls. She even talked about having Bev visit her at her home in Florida, but never followed through on arranging the trip. She still attended the annual meetings at Bev's group home in when she came North in the summer, but she could tell that Jonnie and I had taken charge. She remained involved with Bev's care for about a year or so, but gradually disengaged herself from our family completely and never saw Bev again. In 1998 I officially became Bev's primary family contact and my house became her "home."

Bev was never the same after both her parents were gone. After they passed away her demeanor changed. It didn't happen all at once, but gradually her childlike manner diminished. She was in her early 50's when she lost them, so some of her personality metamorphosis was part of the aging process, but much of it was brought on by the same feeling that all adult children get when they are orphaned. We all have to accept the fact that we are no longer someone's children. We are all grown up and alone in the world. The children that we were fade away as the years without parents pass. Whether or not Bev understands the concept of death doesn't matter. She does understand that her parents have gone away, and she no longer feels like a little girl anymore. She is still loved and cared for, she still comes "home" for holidays and birthdays, but there is no one to call "Mom" and "Dad", no one who can love her quite the same as they did.

Both of my parents loved Bev very much, but expressed that love in very different ways. Like most parents, they each played a different role. My mother was more the caregiver and teacher, my father the joker and philosopher. When my parents were still together, both during the Pennhurst years and after, visits with Bev were filled with tension. They never agreed on how to handle Bev. My mother was much more serious and worried more about Bev's condition and progress or lack of it. My father felt that it was more important to entertain Bev and give her a chance to escape her grim existence. His playfulness only made my mother angry. My mother's anger only made my father more contrary. Bev was continually pulled back and forth between these two attitudes, a circumstance that probably didn't help her unbalanced mental state. After the divorce, when Bev saw one or the other alone instead of together, her visits were far more calm and pleasant for everyone.

When Bev visited her mother at the apartment, everything was orderly, calm, and structured, exactly what Bev needed. She sat quietly, sang, counted, recited nursery rhymes, remembered her manners, and felt relaxed with the predictability of events. No one else could ever make Bev feel as safe and secure as her mother. When Bev visited her father, however, nothing was predictable. The only sure things were lots of candy and lots of fooling around. No one could make Bev laugh like her dad. They both shared the same sly smile and mischievous nature. Bev was the one person in the world who loved my father unconditionally, trusted him and adored him, and expected no more than he gave.

As long as our father was alive, Bev still felt that she had parents. When her dad was still around, she seemed to believe that her mom must be somewhere nearby, too. But when her father passed away, Bev felt lost. She missed her dad terribly and asked for him for years after his death. Dad and Bev had a very special connection that no one else could ever replace. She loved him dearly and never transferred her feelings to any other male the way she could sometimes relate to other females in place of her mother. He carried part of her away with him when he died. A certain light in her went out, and I never saw her laugh again the way she laughed with her dad.

~16~

Peter Pan Principle

On June 11, 1952, when Bev was admitted to Pennhurst, her world began to come apart and spin out of control. Her new life in the institution was a bizarre and frightening landscape, and the home she knew outside the institution underwent disorienting changes as the years went by. After Bev went to live at Pennhurst, the family stayed in the house familiar to her in Mohnton for only two more years, then moved to another house, then another, and another. During all this upheaval her only constant was her parents. Whether together or separate, they were always there for her, even when her homes changed and so many other people in her life came and went. They were her one link to her happier past and her one comfort in her darker present.

I had often wondered why Bev wasn't able to develop a closer relationship to Greg and Jonnie and me, but as I pieced the past together in her story, an answer began to emerge. For Bev, time stood still after June 11, 1952. Her mind's eye would always picture her home as the house in Mohnton. Her parents would always be two beautiful young people who loved her when no one else would and gave her candy and toys and all her favorite things and were synonymous with a place called home. She would always be six years old, and her siblings would always be ten and five and two. In her family picture, no one ever aged. Because she never grew up, in her world we didn't either. So when we all did, in reality, get older and no longer looked the same, we became different people. We are no longer her brother and sisters, but other people with their names. We call ourselves Greg and Rory and Jonnie, but for her we are not the same Greg and Rory and Jonnie who were her siblings. We are just familiar faces who come and go like everyone else.

These days when I show Bev a photograph of our family taken in 1951, she can tell me every name without hesitation, but when I show her a photograph of us taken more recently, she needs to be prompted to identify us correctly. In conversation Bev is rarely able to put two sentences together coherently. Yet, with a little help, she can recite nursery rhymes, sing a repertoire of childhood songs, play patty cake, say the alphabet, and pray the Lord's Prayer before we  eat our meals together. She can do these things because she learned them all from her mother over sixty years ago. That is her reality.

After my parents both passed away and I had to become the primary family member in Bev's life, I took on the role as a responsibility and didn't stop to think about how Bev perceived me. As the years went by and we all settled into a new routine of visitations and regular interactions, I finally started to understand how Bev related to me and Greg and Jonnie. At first I was disturbed by the detachment she showed to us, until I finally got it. Now that I understand, I'm happy to be the person who brings her to a place called home and gives her toys and ice cream and all the favorite things she still can have. I don't mind that she sometimes thinks I'm Mom or someone named Anne. That's where we are today. But at any moment we can travel back in Bev's time machine and be kids again. We can go back there with her and be forever young.

~17~

A Stranger in the Family

Beverley is our sister, yet there are times when she has been like a stranger in the family. For so many years, when Bev attended family gatherings, she came like a visitor rather than a family member. In some respects, that was good. She was treated with special care, as an honored guest. We went out of our way to give her everything she wanted and to make sure she was comfortable and happy. In other ways it was not good, because her status as a guest removed her from the role of a regular family member. Because she came and went, the space she occupied in our family opened up when she was there and closed again when she left. Her time with us was temporary. Truly it was not until our parents passed away that I began to form a new relationship with Bev, that I began to look at her more intimately. She finally became a flesh and blood sister who, little by little, took up permanent residence in my life.

These days, when Bev comes to visit, we always take some quiet time to sit with her and hold her hand and have a chat. When any one of us looks at Bev and asks, "Bevvy, who am I?", she will say one name after another, going through a list stored in her memory. Sometimes the person asking the question is on the list, sometimes not. Names are not important to her - relationships are. There has never been any doubt in her mind about who "mom" and "dad" are, but "sister" and "brother" don't seem to have a tag for her to hold onto. She's really not quite sure what they represent.

How did that come to be so? When I was busy growing up and living my life, I didn't think much about it. Now that I'm older and take time to examine my life more closely, I do wonder how it came to be that way. Our brother Greg, sister Jonnie, and I all have that special connection that biological siblings usually do. Because Greg has lived most of his adult life as a missionary in Brazil, and now that he is back in the States still lives hundreds of miles away, we rarely see each other. Yet even when we haven't been together for long periods of time, we still feel close and pick up conversations as if we had just been talking yesterday. As for Jonnie and me, even though we have long since gotten our AARP cards, we continue to have the enduring "big sister, little sister" relationship of our childhood. But with Bev, we never got a chance to form such bonds. At a young age our sister took a path that led her far away from us, and those vital connections were broken.

Even in the early days when we were all growing up together, Bev didn't seem to be able to develop a close relationship with any of us. Her primary relationship was always with her parents, not us. She never communicated well with other people and spent most of her time in her own world where no one else could follow. When she did interact with us in playtime, she reached out from that world as if through a curtain. We never had a sense of really being together in the same place, in the same time. Games with Bev were never much fun. She got away with hitting and screaming and throwing things, when we would be reprimanded for such behavior. We didn't understand why she didn't have to follow the rules. It just didn't seem fair to us. As young children we couldn't realize that Bev wasn't enjoying such behavior. Though she was suffering inside, we didn't see it that way. To us it seemed that Bev was getting rewarded for being a brat. She was forever throwing tantrums and causing a fuss, she always needed special care and attention, and she made life difficult for everyone else in the house. We felt she was getting more than her fair share of our parents' time. It would take special effort on our part to stop being selfish and learn how to love her, warts and all. Unfortunately, before we were old enough to figure it out, she left for Pennhurst.

Naturally, once Bev left home, any relationship we were to develop with our sister was entirely dependent upon our parents. It was up to them to explain what was so "wrong" with her that she had to go away. It was up to them to make sure that she would remain part of the family with an important place in our lives. The trouble was that our parents weren't good at relationships and neither of them was good at communicating with us. This continuing lack of communication would cause many problems in the family dynamic through the years. We children were left to try to guess at what was going on, to read between the lines and fill in the blanks as best we could. I know for a fact that we filled in those blanks with a lot of misinformation. It would have been so much healthier for all of us if our parents would have had forthright discussions with us, but that never happened. We were pretty much left to try to figure things out on our own.

So much of what we learned about what was happening in our lives was through listening to our parents' conversations, either openly or covertly. Many nights I remember crouching at the top of the steps with Jonnie to listen to our parents having a private conversation downstairs. In the old farmhouse in Sinking Spring we also had another place besides the stairwell to listen when we dared. In our parents' bedroom there was a round hole in the floor with a vent made to allow heat from a space heater or kerosene stove to rise to the second floor. I can still vividly recall Jonnie and me lying on our stomachs and peering down through that vent, which was situated just above the kitchen table. It was a perfect way to spy on our parents when they argued or talked about forbidden matters not for children's ears. There, lying in the dark as quiet as ghosts, we heard many secrets and listened to our mother cry softly. I'm sure, though there were certainly many things for our mother to weep over, some of those tears surely were shed over Bev. We didn't understand most of went on down below us in that kitchen, but we wanted so desperately to know. We did understand that there was an undercurrent of sadness in our house, but we were left to wonder and worry on our own. Our parents literally left us in the dark, not just about Bev, but about so much else.

Neither one of our parents was a good communicator, but for different reasons. Our father was a great talker and a spectacular salesman. He was one of those guys who really could sell ice to the Eskimos. When we were kids we listened to his endless ramblings and empty promises. When I was young I loved to hear him talk. I enjoyed his stories, soaked up his philosophizing, and believed in his dreams. However, by the time we were teenagers, we all got tired of hearing it. I had been let down and disappointed by him countless times. I began to realize that it was all empty talk, self promotion rather than self esteem, wishful thinking rather than dreams, and a pattern of lost opportunities. He was our very own Willy Loman. I began to pity Mother for having to listen to it, and pretend to believe it, for all those years. I didn't understand why he needed to tell those stories or why my mother needed to believe in them.

Mother, on the other hand, talked very little. She expressed very little emotion, turned privacy into an art form, and was stoic to a fault. She always seemed very serious, though she had a brilliant smile. Her life was filled with sadness, so much loss and longing, that I believe she just had to close up and live inside herself. When I was young I was very curious and asked lots of questions of all kinds. I soon learned that personal questions were either not answered at all or brushed aside with limited responses. She often just said she didn't remember. So many times I wondered to myself , "How could she not remember that?" After a while I just stopped asking. Even as an adult there were some subjects that I knew she would not discuss. I think many of her memories were truly repressed and others she simply chose not to talk about.

If it weren't for our eavesdropping, we wouldn't have had a clue what was going on half the time. Mom and Dad never sat down with us to have a family chat. We discussed some things at the dinner table, had a few conversations in the car, but never gathered as a family expressly to have a serious talk. Of course, we grew up in an age where most parents didn't communicate with their children openly. Parents told their kids what they felt they needed to know. As a rule they didn't include them in making decisions and they kept their private lives private. Children were like the characters in the Peanuts comic strip. They went their own way, lived their own lives, and only occasionally heard the distant "blah, blah, blah" of their parents. That's just the way it was. Unfortunately, for families that had difficult situations like ours with Bev, this lack of communication created a dysfunctional family dynamic with lots of suppressed emotions bursting forth in inappropriate ways. Intimate discussions often turned into arguments. Dad ranted, Mom cried. There were many icy silences between them, and dinnertime was often a frosty affair. Luckily, I had Jonnie to help me fill the uncomfortable void with mindless chatter as our parents fumed across the table from each other. On a daily basis, they both protected themselves from their true feelings, our mother with righteous stoicism and hard work, our father with dalliance and drink.

Although our parents were opposites in so many ways, in one respect they were very much alike. For both of them, denial was a way of life. They shared a common response to life's difficulties - if you ignore it, it doesn't exist. If you don't answer the telephone, the creditors will give up calling. If you change your address, the past disappears. If you don't believe something, it's not true. Sometimes denial led to neglect, and neglect often led to tragedy. They both paid the ultimate price In the end, because their denial killed both of them. Our mother ignored the lump that she found in her breast, our father ignored the mole growing on his back. As a result Mother eventually died from breast cancer, and Dad died from melanoma. Neither of them could break their pattern of denial, even when it meant an early death for them both.

When it came to Bev, their ability to ignore reality was put to the acid test. In the beginning I'm sure they truly believed that placing Bev in Pennhurst was the best thing they could do both for her and the rest of us. It must have been a relief for them to be able to focus on the rest of their children while Bev was in the hands of professionals who were going to help her with her problems. Unfortunately, I don't think it was very long before they realized that Pennhurst was creating more problems than it was solving. They had sent Bev down the rabbit hole, but Pennhurst surely wasn't Wonderland. It couldn't have been very long before they realized what a bad decision it had been to send her there. But once the realization hit them, what could they do? They were stuck. Pennhurst was not the place for her, but where could she go? Once her behavior started to become more severe, they couldn't even consider bringing her back home to deal with it. There was nothing to do but leave her there and pray that she would improve somehow. They went into their coping mode. At a loss for what to do, they accepted the situation, and dealt with it by keeping Bev separate from the rest of their lives.

I was four and a half years old when Bev left our home in Mohnton to live at Pennhurst. Even though that is the age when most children begin to be aware of events and to remember them, I don't recall the actual parting or the immediate aftermath. I can't conjure up a picture of a suitcase standing by the door or a tearful goodbye with hugs and kisses. Perhaps my parents tried to make the departure a non event so as not to upset Bev. I can imagine them telling her that she was simply going for a ride in the car. I have no idea what they told us, but however it all happened, it wasn't remarkable enough to have made an impression on me. Her leaving was just another one of those events in my life that left me feeling perplexed and anxious. One day Bev was there, the next she was not. No preparations, no explanations, no consolation. Our sister was simply gone, and that was that.

Although I was too young to remember it, I wonder what it must have been like for us when Bev actually left. I can imagine that at first it must have been almost a relief, that the day to day routine became easier for everyone without constant interruptions and outbursts. It would have been so much more quiet and calm. We children could play and eat and sleep in peace. Our parents would have had more time for us. In fact, one of the reasons Mother gave to the social worker for requesting Bev's admission to Pennhurst was that she had little time for her other children. Taking care of Bev was a full time job. Now, with Bev living at Pennhurst and Greg and me attending school, Mother had only Jonnie to take care of during the day. Perhaps she even had time to waitress more hours and bring in a little extra money. Nevertheless, despite the fact that Bev's absence may have made life easier for them in many ways, there is no doubt that our parents were in emotional agony. Their family was broken.

At first, Greg and I may have had a different point of view. For a while we may actually have enjoyed our more peaceful life without Bev in the house. But as the days and weeks went by and she didn't come back, it became very disturbing, even frightening. How could we possibly comprehend what had happened? Greg would have had some understanding of the concept that Bev was being sent away to a special school. He would have been aware of the preparations, would have watched her leave in the car with our parents. But to me, a four and a half year old child, she might as well have been plucked up by trolls and spirited away. I had no idea what had gone on. A little over two years earlier I had lost a baby brother, when Geoffrey died. Now Bev was gone. My young mind worried. Who might be next?

Right after Bev left home, I don't think I had any concept of what really had occurred. It took me a long while to realize that she wasn't ever going to live with us again. One thing I am sure of is that when that realization finally did hit me, I was afraid. A penetrating fear slowly but surely began to creep in until it took up residence deep inside me, and that fear influenced my life for many years to come. The fear perched on my shoulder like Walt Disney's Jiminy Cricket. Only my fear was not a kindly cricket who whispered advice in my ear. It was a place named Pennhurst, and it whispered not advice, but a warning, - "be good, or else."

My mother was a great one for using euphemisms and skirting the truth. Instead of explaining what mental retardation was and how it affected Bev, she simply told me that Bev wasn't normal and didn't know how to behave like other children. I came to believe that Bev was sent away because she was naughty and went off to a special school to learn how to behave better. She was not normal. Normal people don't act the way she did. I began to worry about being normal, and I tried to behave properly so that I could be normal. I was very cautious about everything I did and said. Be good. Be quiet. Don't make anyone angry. I was careful not to attract attention to myself unless I was very sure that I was doing the right thing and doing it well. Otherwise, I tried to be invisible. I wanted to be normal so that I would not be sent away. To make matters worse, Bev's departure added to the pattern of loss in my young life. My baby brother Geoffrey had developed a rash and died suddenly, my little sister Jonnie had fractured her skull in a car accident and very nearly died, and now my big sister Bev had been taken away to learn how to behave. It was too much. As time went on I became more and more apprehensive about what might happen next.

I became a lifelong worrier. If there is one thing my early life taught me, it's that nothing is certain. One day you lose your brother, one day you lose your sister, one day you lose your house and all your possessions. Nothing is certain and no one is safe. Misfortune hovered over us like a cloud harboring a storm that could strike at any second. I actually learned to hide from misfortune. I believed that if I were very quiet and didn't attract any attention, misfortune would pass me over, not even notice me. I became extremely introverted and reserved.

When Bev came home to visit, her energy was chaotic and I was upset with her. I wanted to tell her to be quiet, stop yelling, stop whining, stop hitting. If you would only behave and be very, very quiet, they would leave you alone. You could come home. You could live under the radar like me. But she wouldn't listen, she didn't understand. I was afraid to be near her, not only because she might hit me, but because I thought I would get pulled into her chaotic energy storm and be swept away with her. Every time she went away again, I was relieved that I was allowed to stay. I was sorry that she was leaving, but I was happy that I was not going with her. I wanted her to stay, but only if she could be quiet. I felt guilty that I couldn't make her understand and I couldn't keep them from taking her away, but I was glad that when she left, she took the chaos with her and the house was quiet again. How could I hide with all that noise? *Great personal disclosure!*

The year after Bev left home, I came close to being killed. I was hit by a car while crossing the street a few blocks from my house and wound up in the hospital with a concussion and a broken leg. I wasn't supposed to cross the street alone, and I felt that I was being punished for my disobedience, especially when a police officer came to the hospital to ask me a lot of questions about what had happened. I was afraid that he had come to put me in jail, broken leg and all, for disobeying my mother. After all, they had taken Bev away for being bad, and now they had called the police about my misbehavior. I can still remember the policeman looming above me like a great blue giant. I was terrified. After a few days in the hospital, I was elated to find out that I was going home and not to jail. Not long after, in September, when I started first grade, I hopped along happily on my crutches to attend my regular school and not the special school for bad children.

There were so many factors that made me a timid and frightened child. As far as I know, neither my brother Greg nor my sister Jonnie developed the kinds of fears that I did. I think a big factor that led to my anxieties was my age at the time all of our family tragedies occurred. I felt overwhelmed by the tumult that was our life in Mohnton. Our brother Geoffrey's death, the automobile accident that almost killed Jonnie, Bev's leaving for Pennhurst, my getting hit by a car, our family bankruptcy and move to the inner city all happened before I was seven years old. At a time of my life when young children are first going out to meet the world, I found the world to be a very hostile place. And at a time when young children need the attention of their parents, my parents' attention was elsewhere. It was not exactly the formula for a happy, confident child.

Besides our insecure family situation, I also had personal problems that made it difficult for me to develop into a well adjusted youngster. I was terribly nearsighted and went through life observing everything around me as a blur. I'm sure that at school my teachers' first impressions were that I was stupid. After a time they finally realized that I was very intelligent, but could not see the chalkboard or much of anything that was more than four feet away. Apparently our parents couldn't afford eyeglasses for me. I did finally get a pair when I was eight years old, but I lost one of the lenses at the playground and it was never replaced. I was fourteen years old before I got another pair of glasses. I will never forget the day I came home from the optometrist wearing my new spectacles. Shortly after I arrived home it began to snow. As I looked out the window, I was astonished and stood watching in fascination. It was the first time in my life that I had ever seen snowflakes.

As a youngster, I was very shy. To add to my nearsightedness, I also had a lazy eye. For reasons unknown to me, our father resisted anyone's recommendations on correcting it, and I lived with the burden of being "cross eyed" for my entire life. Other children made fun of me and adults questioned me about it until I finally decided never to look anyone in the eye again. I spent an entire lifetime looking down or sideways. On top of that, just having to explain my unusual first name embarrassed me terribly. In a world of Linda's and Donna's and Susie's, I was Rory. Every introduction was painful. My odd name made me different. My lazy eye made me different. Having a intellectually disabled sister made me different. I felt like some sort of alien. Every new encounter was a potential embarrassment. Add to this my realization that we were poor and that I had none of the nice clothes or toys that many other children possessed, and my low self esteem is no surprise. How could I be expected to weather the loss of siblings with confidence and security? How could I understand that what happened to Bev was not going to happen to me? How could I believe that everything was going to be fine?

Greg did a much better job of coping than I did. Though he also became withdrawn from his surrounding circumstances, he created a better world for himself. As the firstborn child and the only boy, he held a special position in the sibling hierarchy and had an unusual amount of freedom. When he was a youngster, Mother was busy taking care of Bev, having more babies, and working. She didn't have much time or energy for anything else. Since Bev wasn't much of a playmate, he had to figure out early on how to entertain himself. He was very intelligent and loved to learn new things both in and out of school. He read and drew and painted and played with toys like erector sets and Lincoln Logs. Since life at home could be very chaotic and uncertain, he was happy to retreat into his own fantasy world, staying aloof and keeping family interaction to a minimum. As long as he stayed out of trouble, he was allowed to do pretty much as he pleased. He spent his time riding his bicycle, hanging out with his buddies and playing in the neighborhood, or hiding in his room at home, generally avoiding all three of his sisters as much as possible. He did his part to help look after us when he was asked, but we were girls and didn't really interest him. By the time Bev left home he was ten years old, and he knew something bad was about to happen. He had watched the school principal and the social workers come to the house. He saw that his father was angry and his mother upset. He listened to the grown ups talk about a place called Pennhurst, but since it had nothing to do with him, he didn't worry much about it.

Jonnie, the baby of the family, had the least contact with Bev. She's seven years younger than Bev and didn't ever get the experience of being her sister at home. She was only 1 1/2 years old when Bev left for Pennhurst, and her earliest memories of her would come later when she visited a strange looking girl in a crazy place. She doesn't remember the pretty, lively older sister who lived with us in the big house in Mohnton. I was really the only sister she knew. The bald and battered person who lived in the smelly, noisy institution wasn't the same sort of sister at all. It isn't any wonder that Jonnie's attitude toward Bev would be completely different from Greg's or mine. Because she never got a chance to relate to Bev at home, her departure would not have made much of a difference in her young life. She was busy learning to walk and talk and, like most toddlers, was just beginning to learn about the world around her. She had suffered a fractured skull in the car accident, and was carefully watched and doted on during her recovery. If anything, Bev would have seen her as a competitor for Mother's attention. Jonnie says that she never really looked at Bev as a sister at all. By the time she would have understood what a sister really is, Bev would have been long gone from the household. If Bev had been a normal sibling, the seven year difference in age between her and Jonnie would have made their relationship a Big Sister/Little Sister one in which Bev would have been expected to be a mentor and caretaker. That certainly was a role Bev could never fulfill. For all intents and purposes, Jonnie had only one sister, and that was me.

As I was growing up, I also felt that I really had only one sister. When people I met asked me if I had brothers and sisters, I would tell them about Greg and Jonnie, but I rarely mentioned Bev. Mentioning Bev would only have prompted people to ask more questions that I didn't want to answer and didn't know how to answer. There also were occasions when our mother specifically told us not to mention Bev and, as a result, I felt it was safer not to mention her at all rather than try to guess when it was permitted and when it was not. At the time I didn't realize that it wasn't Bev that was the taboo subject, it was Pennhurst. Talking about Bev meant talking about Pennhurst, something no one wanted to do. Mother was forever telling us not to mention this or that. Her penchant for privacy became a family trait. I certainly adopted it and have always been uncomfortable with answering personal questions. I still rarely discuss details of my life with anyone but my closest friends, and only a few of them know about Bev. Even my lifelong best friend didn't know about her until we were adults. Bev was not part of our daily family life. Since our friends and acquaintances never saw her, it was easy to ignore her existence.

By 1955, when the family had settled into the farmhouse in Sinking Spring, Bev's absence was firmly established. She had already been living at Pennhurst for three years by that time. Greg was thirteen years old, entering his adolescence, and drifting even further away from his siblings. He had a wild imagination and developed an oddball sense of humor. As he grew older, he loved building things, as well as taking things apart to find out how they worked. He was extremely creative, both artistically and mechanically, and could spend hours with his own projects. Jonnie and I don't remember seeing much of him during these years. He spent most of his time in his room experimenting like some mad wizard or off exploring the wider world with his friends. He tried his best to avoid the family drama as much as possible. Who could blame him? As soon as he turned fourteen he began working. His first job was at a popular local ice cream store where we loved to visit him and wolf down huge ice cream sundaes. Between school and work and running around with his teenage friends, he was busy with his own life and didn't much concern himself with Jonnie and me. Though he was supposed to be in charge, he wasn't home very much and Jonnie and I were pretty much on our own. Our parents both worked and were in and out of the house on different shifts. We were expected to take care of ourselves and stay out of trouble. Don't burn the house down, don't get lost, don't break anything, and be home for supper at 5:00. While our parents were gone, Greg ruled the roost, but when he was not around, we were on our own.

During the years in Sinking Spring the family visited Bev fairly regularly at Pennhurst and she still visited with us at home. Though Jonnie and I accompanied our parents to Pennhurst, Greg didn't go. At that time he would have been working on weekends and wouldn't have had much free time. In the summer, when Bev visited at home, Greg would also have been working and not at home very much. Since Bev was also a teenager by then, she was becoming a young woman and had even less in common with her brother than ever. And, while Greg was growing up and morphing into an adult, Bev remained stuck in the time warp of Pennhurst. They continued to drift further and further apart until their fragile bond was eventually broken.

Most of Jonnie's memories of Bev come from that time when we lived in Sinking Spring and saw Bev the most frequently. Those were the years when we started to accompany our parents to Pennhurst to visit Bev there. I was eight years old, Jonnie five, when we first went down and waited outside the gates for our parents to bring Bev out. Later, when we got a bit older, we started to go inside the grounds and had our Fellini like experiences within the bizarre atmosphere of Pennhurst. Being younger than I was, she didn't internalize the experience like I did, but looked at it more like a strange sideshow that she couldn't quite comprehend. To her, Bev was one of those odd people who lived in that weird place that had little to do with her life back home. Because Jonnie never got to know her as a member of our family, Bev never really had a significant place in her life.

By the time Jonnie was old enough to have any real understanding about what was going on with Bev, our contact with her had become less and less frequent. When she was ten years old we moved to Wyomissing, where we both eventually graduated from high school. Bev had stopped coming home for visits and our trips to Pennhurst had become voluntary. Bev had become a loud, hyperactive teenager who had little interest in her siblings. In that regard, the feeling was somewhat mutual. Even though we still went to Pennhurst occasionally, we did it only as an obligation. She had nothing to do with our day to day lives. Both Jonnie and I were entering our own teenage years by then and our relationship with her was not a priority.

Once I had entered my teens, I started to be more aware of other people's reactions to the fact that I had a intellectually disabled sister. I started to notice a judgmental aspect to their curiosity about her. A red flag went up in my mind and I decided to avoid the discomfort completely by not mentioning her at all.

There were many reasons why I was happy to hide having Bev as my sister. The most overwhelming reason was fear. I was always afraid that her mental condition was genetic and that any one of us could also have that "crazy" gene inside us. I worried about it constantly. Since our father's behavior was often outlandish, it reinforced the impression that mental illness was part of our family. He was an emotional, unpredictable, unreliable rascal who delighted in using colorful language and actually seemed to enjoy embarrassing us in public. In many ways he was, indeed, mentally unstable. Unfortunately, I was an adult before I realized that much of his unacceptable behavior was caused by his drinking. I would have worried a lot less had I known. As a child I was hesitant to mention having a mentally handicapped sister, not only because I couldn't answer people's questions about her, but because I feared that they would think that there was something wrong with me, too.

As the years went by, I watched my big sister transform from a beautiful little girl into a bald, toothless zombie. To see what mental disability could do to a person, to experience what a mental institution was like, and to realize what society thought about the intellectually disabled, all made me terrified of mental illness and made me irrationally afraid of going insane. I didn't understand the difference between mental retardation and mental illness. To me they were one in the same. This unfortunate misconception turned ordinary anxiety into a state of panic that would cause me great heartache later in my adult years.

Quite frankly, as a teenager I was embarrassed by having a mentally handicapped sister. Such a sibling was not "normal", and I was desperately trying to be as normal as possible. Like most teenagers I didn't want to attract any negative attention to myself. To make matters worse, the community we lived in during my high school years was a very exclusive society and my family didn't fit in to begin with. I was the classic high school outsider. An academic nerd, a wallflower with a lazy eye and crooked teeth, economically deprived and unworldly, I was low on the social food chain. The last thing I wanted to do was give anyone another excuse to ostracize me. Revealing the presence of a sister in a state hospital would have provided more fodder for ridicule and certainly wouldn't have raised my social standing one bit.

Jonnie, however, had a different attitude than I did about talking about Bev to other people. Though she didn't go out of her way to talk about her intellectually disabled sister, she didn't think it was a taboo subject either. In high school Jonnie was cute, perky, well liked, and had lots of friends. She's not one for keeping secrets and, indeed, has a penchant for telling all. As a rule she didn't feel the need to hide Bev's existence from her friends. When she was asked about brothers and sisters, she usually included Bev without thinking much about it. It's easy to understand why Jonnie was more comfortable talking about Bev. Since she was still a baby when Bev left home, she wasn't traumatized by the event. She didn't develop the same concerns that I had about being sent away for bad behavior, nor my morbid fear of mental illness. She didn't feel any close connection with Bev, let alone think she might be like her in some way. Since, as the baby of the family she always had our brother and me to rely on, her early childhood was a lot less emotionally stressful than Greg's and mine had been. While Greg and I had learned at an early age that we had to look out for ourselves, Jonnie had the advantage of being the baby with two older siblings to take care of her. By the time she was old enough to know what was really going on in the world around her, our family circumstances had stabilized a great deal. Bev was fading out of the family picture, and Jonnie more or less took it as a simple matter of fact.

Greg, Jonnie, and I each had a different way of dealing with it, according to our own personalities and our positions in the family order. Greg, the favored firstborn son, clever and independent, separated himself from the family as much as possible and became a maverick, immersing himself in creative pursuits and coming and going as he pleased. I, the overlooked middle child, quiet and shy, internalized much of what went on, withdrew into my own world of imagination and fantasy, and tried to protect myself by being as good as I could possibly manage. Jonnie, the sweet baby, uncomplicated and open, felt no reason to hide anything from the world, and innocently accepted our family as it was.

After just a few years in Pennhurst the damage to Bev had been done. The "school" that was supposed to help her had turned her, instead, into a frightened and unruly institutional being, battered both physically and mentally. These changes were upsetting for the whole family. However, I don't believe that my parents had any idea how seriously affected the rest of us children were. Though Beverley's bruises on her face and arms were painfully evident, ours were hidden below the surface, leaving emotional scars that no one could see at the time. Beverley was the one with mental retardation. We were healthy. What did we have to worry about? No one was concerned about us.

These days there would be family counseling available to help the siblings to cope with having a intellectually disabled sister, but in those days there was little help for the disabled themselves, let alone the healthy siblings. When I was in elementary school, there were no counselors for students. The school nurse patched up cuts and took temperatures. Doctors came in to give eye tests and polio vaccine. We were weighed and measured. Mental health was not their concern. In high school we had a guidance counselor whose main duties were giving out college pamphlets and dealing with students who sneaked out to smoke cigarettes. I would never have thought of going to him with a personal problem. I would doubt that he had the professional training to do much more than give an occasional pep talk or dole out routine textbook advice.

A family doctor might have been able to give some advice, but for most of our lives we didn't have one. Mother mentioned taking us to a doctor when we were toddlers, but once we had had our childhood immunizations, we never went to the doctor except for emergencies. We literally had to be on Death's doorstep to receive medical attention. When I was a toddler and fell off my tricycle, I did get stitches for a nasty gash in my wrist. The doctor was called to the house when our baby brother Geoffrey had an allergic reaction and ultimately died. Jonnie needed follow up care after she fractured her skull in a car accident. I went to the hospital for appointments after I broke my leg. Other than that, we never saw a doctor. Dad didn't believe in them. He felt that all you needed to do to stay healthy was take vitamins and pray. After my broken leg was healed at the age of six, I didn't see a doctor again until I went to college. No checkups, no preventive medicine, and certainly no psychological counseling.

Though the schools didn't provide any help and we didn't have a family doctor, we did attend church regularly and might have expected some guidance from that source. However, as active and involved as our family was with our church, the pastor never counseled us. Though he may have talked with my parents about Bev, he never spoke to us children about our relationship with our sister. I remember him as an outgoing and charismatic man whom we loved and respected, and I, for one, would have welcomed a few reassuring words from him. Nevertheless, that church was a place where I always felt safe and happy, where everything was good. Even without formal counseling, it did bring our family closer together, helped us to cope, and reassured us that all would be well.

Though I can understand that there was no professional help available, there was also a remarkable lack of support from anyone in our extended family. It's true that we didn't have a large family to draw upon, and we were certainly not what you would call closely knit. On our father's side we had a grandfather and step grandmother, our great aunt Ruth, and "Aunt" Florence. Our father had a step brother whom we never met, even though he lived not far away. On my mother's side we had a grandmother, our Uncle Joe and his wife Sophie, and our three cousins - Johnny, Joe, and David. There were never any big family gatherings where everyone mingled. As a matter of fact, I don't believe the two sides of the family ever even spoke to each other. On Sundays after church we would rotate visiting the various relatives separately, but I don't recall any of those visits involving Bev. They might sometimes ask how she was getting along at Pennhurst. As for the rest of us, we were politely asked how we were doing in school or what we had gotten for Christmas. There were no warm and fuzzy hugs or cozy chats. The visits were mostly for the grown ups to catch up on family news. Once the perfunctory greetings were over, we children went off and to play and ignored the conversation.

I don't really know how much our parents talked about Bev with our relatives or how much advice or help any of them gave to them. Many of the conversations around the table after lunch or over cocktails in the living room certainly included discussions about Bev, but I wasn't privy to them. I only know what I saw and heard myself from the perspective of a youngster. For the most part they all adopted the prevailing attitude of the day that once a child was sent away to an institution, she was no longer included in the family circle. It was sad, but it couldn't be helped. Best forget about it and go on with your life.

When I think back to all the holiday gatherings through our early years, I can picture the family gathered around at one house or the other, and none of those mental pictures include Bev. No Bev opening Christmas gifts, no Bev in a Halloween costume, no Bev coloring Easter eggs. There are so many blank spaces in our family life that should have been filled with memories of Bev. For instance, in all the years when I was living at home, I don't remember making cards or gifts for her, or ever personally giving her a gift of my own choosing. I don't remember writing her letters or drawing her pictures. These are all activities that I would consider normal for a sibling of a mentally handicapped sister living away from home in an institution, yet I remember nothing of the sort happening.

When she came home from Pennhurst for her visits I don't remember hugging her or holding her hand or playing with her. Instead, I do recall being frightened by her behavior to the point of avoiding being near her. Since Mother and Dad continued to treat her with the special care that separated her from the rest of us, she never quite fit into the daily family routines. Somehow she remained an outsider. The very fact that I have to wrack my brains to picture Bev interacting with the family is very telling in itself. And it's not just me. Greg and Jonnie have few concrete images either. Jonnie is the best at childhood recollections, but even she has difficulty recalling memories of Bev. The fact that all three of us have trouble remembering her says so much about Bev's place, or rather lack of it, in the family. It is this mystery of her shadowy existence that first nudged at me to write her story, as if by doing so I could in some way make her more real and give her a place in the family album where she belongs.

Once Bev was an adult and had undergone her transformation, we could finally start to enjoy her company. We were adults, too, no longer tangled up in the Miller family angst. In 1984, when Bev stepped out of the institution and into a community living arrangement, we had many more opportunities to interact with her and to relate to her in a new way. She seemed more like a real person once she was living in a group home setting, and we had the chance to get together with Bev like a family, either at Mother's apartment or at Dad's house. Occasionally we even went to see her in her group home. At that time, our parents were the ones who worked in cooperation with Threshold to make sure that she was well cared for and spending more time with her family. We siblings, even though we were seeing her more often, were able to leave everything else up to our parents and go about our lives without really dealing with the details. Even as adults we continued to maintain a certain passivity toward our sister, as if we were still children with no responsibility for her at all. This passivity extended to all our relations with Bev and was something that was difficult to change, even later when we became the caretakers. *Great detail here :*

That strange disconnect exhibited itself in many ways. There is a certain example that stands out in my memory. One Thanksgiving, after our parents passed away, I had the traditional family gathering at my house. As the meal began, people were helping themselves to food, which was laid out on the sideboard, and bringing it back to their seats at a long table. As hostess I was scurrying back and forth setting out food and pouring drinks. When I finally had a chance to sit down at the table, I saw that Bev was sitting patiently in front of an empty plate while everyone else had begun eating. Apparently no one had thought of filling a plate for her. I couldn't believe my eyes as I watched the others eating and conversing as if she weren't even there. As I took her plate and filled it and cut her meat for her, I was annoyed, even angry. But after Bev was happily eating and I looked around the table, my anger turned to sadness. Bev was simply invisible, as she always had been. No one meant to neglect her - it was just someone else's job to look after her.

It wasn't until I retired from my job as an elementary school librarian and had time to reflect on many aspects of my own life that I began to look at Bev differently. It was only then that I began to wonder about what made Bev tick, about what her life away from her family for so many years had been like, about how she had influenced our family dynamic and about how her experience had affected us all psychologically and emotionally. I felt a new connection to her that I had never felt before. I began to see the similarities rather than the differences between us. I realized that, although the three of us had always believed that Bev was not part of our lives, we were very wrong. She is, and always has been, very much a part of us.

A Stanger in the Family

Though Greg, Jonnie, and I are each unique individuals, we are also all alike in many ways. Despite our differences, we are also all the same, and we share an unbreakable bond of sibling loyalty and affection. All three of us have the same eccentric way of looking at life, and we all have the same quirky sense of humor. Against tough odds, we have all turned out pretty much okay. Better than okay, really. You can't grow up with a special person like Bev in the family and not be kind of special yourself. No one who has a intellectually disabled sibling can not be profoundly affected by that relationship. No one who has ever been to a place like Pennhurst can ever look at the world like everyone else. You can never forget how lucky you are. You can never turn a blind eye to the suffering of others. You can never think you are better than anyone else. You can never stop thanking God for your healthy children. You learn to be patient. You learn to be humble. You learn to laugh at just about anything. You learn to let go. There but for the grace of God go we, and there by the grace of God goes Bev.

~18~

Now

For Bev, family was everything. Her life revolved around us and her memories of us. Mom, Dad, her eternally young brother and sisters and, especially, home. Home is a place of safety and security and love, a place that does not confuse her or frighten her, a place that provides the familiarity and routine that her mental condition demands. As a child, when she lived at home with her family, that was the only place she wanted to be. Even before she went away to Pennhurst, she wanted to go home whenever she was tired of being out in the world, whether it was school or church or a doctor's office. But at Pennhurst it became an obsession. While she lived there, going home was all she thought about, twenty four hours a day. It became her mantra. "I go home. I go home. I go home."

To Bev, however, going home has always meant more than being in a particular place. It meant getting away from an uncomfortable or unhappy situation. It was her way of saying that she was overwhelmed. She repeats it over and over again to comfort herself. "I go home for Easter, I go home for Christmas, I go home for Thanksgiving, I go home for my birthday." Nowadays she repeats it out of habit, but in her Pennhurst days I believe it was her lifeline to reality. It filled her tortured mind with thoughts of mother and father, brother and sisters, her own bed, the foods she loved, peace and quiet. For Bev "home" is not so much a physical place as it is the memory of a place, the way it was before Pennhurst.

Now that our parents are gone, I have become Bev's center. I have taken over the duties of a parent and my house is the "home" she comes to. I make sure there are always birthday cakes and Christmas gifts and Easter eggs and holiday feasts. When Bev comes for the holidays, there is usually an assortment of other people around as well. Sometimes the atmosphere can be very busy, with people coming and going, food being prepared, music being played, dogs running around, and all sorts of holiday commotion. We take turns sitting and talking with her, singing songs, and helping her put puzzles together. Even though Bev generally likes a calm environment, I think she enjoys all the stimulation of the family gatherings. Much of the time she just watches and listens, smiling to herself as she counts her quarters and blurts out requests for food and drink. Jonnie and I try to find quiet moments just to hold her hand or talk quietly to her about her favorite things and ask her questions we wish she could answer but never will.

Bev has become a fixture at holiday celebrations at my house. She's an important part of our family get togethers and we couldn't imagine not having her with us. Yet when she is here, most people don't interact very much with her. For the most part, Jonnie and I, and sometimes my husband, are the only ones that have more than cursory contact with her. I have thought about this and have come to the conclusion that unless you have a "past" with her, it is very difficult to have a "present". Bev lives in another world and only occasionally takes a few moments to step into ours. Her reactions to her environment are brief. She will answer a question, follow a direction, look quickly at something, then pop right back into her own mind. It's as if she were attached to a rubber band that sometimes we can stretch toward us, but will always pull her back into her natural, comfortable place when we let go.

As she moves from one world to the next, the expression on her face changes. When we talk about the past, familiar names and places and experiences from her childhood, she smiles, even gets a twinkle in her eyes. When you ask her how old she is, she says she is six, and being six is what makes her happy. Perhaps like Christopher Robin in "Now We Are Six", she lives in her own Hundred Acre Wood populated by her versions of Pooh and Piglet and Eeyore, a world where nothing changes and where everything is as it should be.

BEV

Bev's conversation is very limited. Her speech consists of a lot of repetition and nonsense. Her two favorite subjects are food and coming home and she has lists that she goes over and over. All of us have heard the lists countless times. "I go home for Easter." (Repeat for birthday, Thanksgiving, Christmas, and any other holiday she can think of). "I like cheese." "I want licorice." "Gimmee ice tea." "Chocolate ice cream with chocolate syrup." "I want money, Hon." And on and on. They are each a kind of mantra, not meant so much for communication as for comfort. She is on a never-ending search for a home only remembered and these are the keys to finding it. By repeating those words she is hanging on to some sort of reality. When she gets wrapped up in her lists we try to redirect her, but she never strays far from them.

Her forays into actual communication are brief. Bev engages in echolalia, which means that she repeats what you say to her rather than giving an answer to a question or generating a new thought. Whenever she is unable to process a piece of information or a question, she resorts to echolalia. "Yes" or "no" questions are usually more successfully answered, though she usually tries to comply with an affirmative. Even so, she understands when she is being teased. If you asked her, "Hey, Bev, would you like to go to the moon?", she would answer with a sly smile and a quick "yeah" that seems to challenge you to actually make it happen. Trying to find out what Bev really wants or needs or is thinking can be a guessing game for us. For her, trying to communicate can be a frustrating experience and sometimes causes her great anxiety, which leads her to whine or become agitated. Those of us who know her well can redirect and calm her. Casual acquaintances stay in the safety zone of repetition.

As a rule Bev seems unable to express what she's thinking. Every once in a while she says a whole sentence unprompted. On the rare occasions when that happens, we all stop and stare in surprise. Often the things she says make us laugh because of their whimsy or blunt observation. Those rare glimpses of lucidity make me believe that she is capable of more meaningful communication, but it would take a lot of time and patience to get her thoughts to organize themselves and come out as words. Someone would have to work with her in short sessions several times a day to make a difference, but I would bet that she could have been taught to express herself more fully. I would love to know more about what she remembers, what she knows, and how she feels. It's hard for Jonnie and me, in particular, to sit with her, wanting to talk together, and having so little we can say to each other. In the short amount of time we usually have with her, however, there is very little chance of our being able to make any real breakthroughs in our attempts to communicate with her.

One subject we can never broach is Pennhurst. As much as I would love to talk to her about what she remembers, I stay well away from trying to discuss it. Whenever Pennhurst is mentioned Bev whines, "I don't want to go back to Pennhurst" and becomes upset. As far as she knows, that place is still waiting for her with its maze of tiled hallways, grated windows, chaotic day room, frantic dining hall, and cramped living quarters. Repetitive phrases like "pull my teeth out" and "give me a shot" originated from her experiences there. If Bev has nightmares, they are surely about Pennhurst. I refuse to ask her to relive even one more moment of it.

One of the positive things Bev brought away with her from Pennhurst is her enjoyment of music. Bev loves music of all kinds, but

has a special fondness for Elvis Presley and the Oldies. She is definitely a fan of good old rock and roll music and can sing along with many of the lyrics. It's interesting to note that when Bev takes part in a conversation she uses only the briefest sentences, such as "I want cheese," using as few words as possible to communicate, yet she can sing long passages of lyrics easily and, with a little prompting, can get through an entire song. She has a sense of rhyme and will substitute other rhyming words in a song if she forgets the correct ones. She also has a great sense of rhythm and can clap along with a tune and continue to sing her nonsense syllables in time with the beat. Most of all she loves to dance. Either alone or with a partner she will swing and sway to the music and do something like the Twist combined with the Bristol Stomp. Dancing is one thing that is sure to bring a smile to her face and even get her laughing. Years ago when she was quite overweight it was best to stand well away when she was in full gear on the dance floor. Nowadays she is a bit more subdued, but her love of music is one thing that always brings her pleasure and helps her connect with people around her.

Bev also loves money, especially quarters and small change. One of her mantras is "quarter, quarter, nickel, nickel, dime, dime." This is primarily because coins magically release the contents of vending machines. Like so many other working people, her favorite times of the day when she had a job on the production line were breaks and lunchtime. She hoarded her coins to use in the vending machines to get sodas, candy, and snacks. Although she no longer has a job, she still remembers the days when she could get sodas from the machine at workshop, and she saves up her money just in case. Bev considers every quarter ever minted to be her own personal property and seeking them out is a never ending quest. Once they are in her possession, she guards them carefully and she will not part with the contents of her change purse. She often entertains herself by sitting quietly and counting her coins like a modern day Midas, often giggling as she drops the coins into her purse one by one to hear them clink as they fall.

She carries a pocketbook with her at all times. The contents consist primarily of a comb, the latest greeting cards she has received in the mail, and her coin purse. Her handbags endure some rough treatment being dragged hither and yon, and she goes through quite a few of them in a year's time. She loves her purses, not only because they hold her money, but also because when she was at Pennhurst one of her positive reinforcements was the privilege of carrying a purse. To Bev, carrying a purse means that she is being good, and being good is very important to her. That is why we are always careful to make sure she always has her handbag, and we never try to take it away from her even when she goes into the bathroom. This positive association with money and purses also extends to shopping. Bev loves to shop and doesn't mind parting with the money necessary to buy the things she wants. I believe her love of shopping also comes from her days at Pennhurst when getting to shop at the canteen was another reward for good behavior. Even so, she doesn't always shop for herself. She understands the concept of gift giving and is happy to buy presents for family and friends.

Another thing that Bev truly loves is fingernail polish. Again, getting her nails painted was one of her rewards for good behavior when she was at Pennhurst, so that having polish on her nails reminds her what a good girl she is. There was a period of time when the staff stopped applying polish because she was in the habit of biting at it and eating it, but they eventually gave in and she's been wearing it again. When Bev went to aqua therapy one of her aides used to paint her nails bright colors so that she could follow her hands while swimming. The brighter the color the better, and red is her favorite. Bev also loves getting her hair done. Hair is very important to her since, for a very long time while at Pennhurst, her head was shaved to keep her from pulling her hair out. Those days are long behind her, but having her hair done and combing her hair still make her feel special.

Bev always looks good. She has a closet full of clothes and the staff always makes sure that she is dressed in pretty outfits when she goes out for the day. Her wardrobe has changed many times because of her weight fluctuations, but no matter what her weight, she has always been well dressed. Keeping Bev looking well groomed isn't easy. She spills food and dribbles drink on herself quite frequently and takes little care as to where she steps or sits. Putting herself back together after using the bathroom is also not a priority, and she emerges untucked and rumpled. She also is forever losing gloves or hats or scarves or other accessories. As much as she treasures her handbags, she manages to lose those as well. Those that don't get lost get worn out from being opened and closed so often and from spending a good deal of time on the floor. She can begin a visit with us looking like she just stepped off a fashion runway and leave looking like she's been in a wrestling match.

Bev's favorite activity, by far, is eating. She loves to eat, and when she isn't eating, she loves to talk about eating. She will recite her favorite menu for you with no hesitation - licorice, cheese and ice tea top her list, followed closely by baked beans, spaghetti, and chocolate ice cream with chocolate syrup. Peanut butter and candy of any kind, but particularly chocolate, are also top choices. Tragically, in December of 2008 Bev developed a health problem that makes eating more difficult. She was with us on Christmas Day and the very next day wound up in the hospital with pneumonia, even though we saw no evidence of her being unwell during her visit. During her lengthy hospital stay she received intravenous antibiotics and underwent intensive testing, including a surgical lung biopsy. Afterwards the doctors concluded that she had aspirated food particles into her lungs, causing infection and resulting in pneumonia. Since then she has been hospitalized repeatedly with aspiration pneumonia and has received massive doses of intravenous antibiotics. Each bout takes a heavy toll on her and it gets harder each time for her to recover and get her strength back.

There are several reasons why she might aspirate food. She eats and drinks very quickly, a habit developed long ago in Pennhurst where eating fast was a necessity. Besides eating quickly, she doesn't chew her food thoroughly because she has no teeth. Her teeth were all pulled at Pennhurst when she was only 24 years old. Although she manages very well without teeth, it is difficult for her to chew properly. Dentures are not an option, since Bev simply would not keep them in her mouth. The most significant reason for aspirating, though, is her chronic cough. Bev has had lung problems for years and suffers from repeated bouts of bronchitis. As a result she has a deep cough that can come on in suddenly in persistent bursts. If she begins to cough while she is eating, food or saliva can easily be drawn into her trachea and down into her lungs. Her extreme acid reflux, called GERD, causes her to vomit periodically, adding to the likelihood of aspirating food particles.

In order to prevent this aspiration of food particles, her doctors occasionally revisit the idea of placing a feeding tube directly into her small intestine. If that were done, all her nutrients would be administered through the tube and Bev would never again be allowed to eat by mouth. After much thought Greg, Jonnie, and I decided against such a procedure. We simply cannot imagine not allowing Bev to have food. She is always good natured and cooperative with all the medical procedures she has to endure. But how can we ask her to give up her beloved food and drink? How can we tell her she can never have ice cream or peanut butter or chocolate again? We decided to try to do everything possible to avoid that unthinkable outcome. We and her wonderful staff worked out a plan with the doctors to modifying her eating regime. In order to cut down on the likelihood of aspirating food particles while eating, Bev now eats a strictly pureed diet and drinks liquids that are thickened to the consistency of nectar. She is encouraged to eat slowly and swallow carefully. Now all her food must be pureed and all liquids must be thickened in an attempt to prevent the aspiration of food. Everyone also coaches her to eat slowly and chew thoroughly before swallowing.

She's had to give up many foods, but some, like oatmeal and applesauce and ice cream, she can still have in their natural state. Her beloved licorice is definitely off the list. However, with close monitoring she can continue to enjoy the act of eating and drinking and can appreciate the taste of food, if not the texture. She can still chatter away about food and fantasize about all the wonderful things she might be able to eat. Unfortunately, every few months, despite everyone's best efforts, she still has episodes of aspiration and needs medical intervention. Pureeing her food and thickening her drinks makes her visits home a bit more difficult, but she can still sit down with the family at the table and enjoy eating with us even if she can't have everything she wants. Just being able to be with us to share a meal makes her very happy, no matter what is on her plate.

Bev has a long and complicated medical history. While she was at Pennhurst she was hospitalized several times for illnesses, injuries, and surgeries. Most of her medical needs were taken care of at Pennhurst, though for her surgeries she was taken to nearby Philadelphia hospitals. At various times she was treated for serious gastrointestinal problems, a prolapsed rectum, a benign cyst in one of her breasts, and periodic dental problems. In addition, there were times when she needed to be stitched and bandaged as a result of injuries she acquired during her violent outbursts. She still bears the scars of lacerations she caused herself by banging her head on the walls or the ground. During a fit of frustration, she once put her hand through a window and cut herself seriously. For years she also used to bite her arms, which caused ugly bruises. As a result of her violent behaviors, her accidental injuries, and her illnesses, Bev spent a good amount of time in the infirmary during her residence at Pennhurst. Much of her medical care there was emergency care, while preventive care was minimal until the last few years before she left. Once she went into a community living arrangement, however, she received excellent medical care and began to see a team of doctors on a regular basis.

One of her biggest health problems when she first left the institution was her obesity. Keeping Bev's weight in check was a difficult task. She has always loved to eat, and candy and sodas were her favorite foods. Sweets were often used both as a reward for good behavior and as a way to keep Bev calm. Besides food, some of the medications Bev needed to take also had a tendency to make her put on extra pounds. As a result, for most of her adult life she had a battle with her weight. It took a lot of effort on everyone's part to win the battle. Finally, after being put on a low fat, low carb diet as well as an exercise plan that included swimming, bowling, walking the treadmill, and riding an exercise bike, she gradually lost weight until she finally achieved a healthy size. Ironically, with the additional medical problems she has developed in recent years, she has actually lost too much weight and needs supplements to help her stay at a healthy weight. As she continues to age she has become a mere wisp of her former self.

Though obesity is no longer a problem, through the years after her release from Pennhurst she has developed a long list of health issues and has been in the hospital on numerous occasions. She had her gall bladder removed, a pancreatic pseudocyst removed, and another rectal prolapse surgery. Her chronic conditions include anemia, asthma, hypothyroidism, and gastrointestinal esophageal reflux disease, or GERD, which is an acute form of acid reflux that causes ulceration of the esophagus. This ulceration has resulted in a disorder called Barrett's Esophagus. Stomach acids and food can back up into her esophagus, which contributes to her ongoing episodes of aspiration pneumonia. A hernia which puts pressure on the base of the esophagus also complicates that situation. A couple of years ago she was also diagnosed with Type II diabetes and has been put on a low carb diet to help to manage it. Added to her digestive ailments are her respiratory problems. For many years she had recurrent bouts of bronchitis. To help keep her lungs from becoming congested, she uses a nebulizer several times a day, gets oxygen treatments at night, and sleeps in an adjustable bed with a raised head to help her to breathe easier while sleeping.

A less critical, but nonetheless important, health issue is Bev's sight. She has been nearsighted all her life and was first prescribed glasses when she was not yet four years old. When Mother first took Bev to the Reading Hospital for evaluation the doctors noticed that she held objects very close to her face to study them. Needless to say, it would have been difficult for the doctors to examine Bev to find out exactly what her vision problems were. Nevertheless, an ophthalmologist finally was able to prescribe eyeglasses and Mother somehow got her to wear them most of the time. At Pennhurst she went without glasses for 32 years. After Pennhurst, she had glasses but rarely wore them. She didn't like them and would need constant supervision to keep them on. I have to wonder how correct her prescription really was. Maybe the glasses made her vision worse when she wore them, or maybe Bev was just so accustomed to seeing a blurry world that she didn't feel comfortable seeing clearly. Since I have also been nearsighted all my life, I know what it's like to have blurred vision, and I know that it's something you can get used to. After all those years of blurry vision, Bev developed cataracts as she aged. Very recently she underwent cataract surgery and can now see clearly. After the surgery her eyes opened wider and give her the appearance of being more alert and in touch with her surroundings. Her improved vision makes it possible for her to engage more actively with her environment and with other people. This newfound ability to interact more with the world around her seems to support my theory that her impaired eyesight increased her isolation, making it difficult for her to understand much of what was going on around her and even to communicate with other people.

As one would expect, Bev's psychiatric dossier is long and complicated as well. Her primary diagnoses are for mental retardation, bi-polar disorder, explosive disorder, and obsessive compulsive disorder as well as Tourette syndrome. She needs to take some powerful drugs to keep these disorders in check. It is a balancing act that her doctors monitor carefully. As long as she's medicated properly she is pleasant and happy and easy going. When the medications get out of balance, things can go very wrong and she can become combative and obsessive and loud. Her doctors have periodically tried to reduce her medications because of the side effects, but they have found that she needs a certain minimum level of drug maintenance that can't be tampered with. As a result, she needs to take even more medication to combat some of the side effects, such as involuntary bodily movements. People who take anti psychotic drugs often exhibit such movements with names like tardive dyskinesia and extra pyramidal reaction. Bev has been taking anti psychotic drugs for decades and the physical side effects can be very serious. All of her conditions, both physical and mental, demand the use of a laundry list of medications and at present she is taking over a dozen different drugs.

Modern medicine now has names for Bev's mental conditions and drugs have been developed to help control them, but when Bev was first seen by doctors 65 years ago, they didn't have these diagnoses at their disposal. Mental retardation and mental illness were mysterious conditions that were treated with what now look like very primitive methods. As a result, the Beverley who presented herself to doctors all those years ago isn't the same Beverley who came out of Pennhurst and who lives in a group home today. Much of what Bev became is the result of her institutionalization and the lack of treatment for the conditions she originally suffered from. Today the doctors give her the best life they can while dealing with the results of years of mismanagement and over medication. Considering everything Bev has been through she is doing miraculously well, both physically and emotionally. Her current team of doctors does an amazing job.

Sometimes there are moments, however, that remind us that no matter how cheerful and happy Bev may seem, her demons still lie dangerously close to the surface. About ten years ago her psychiatrist tried to reduce the levels of her psychotropic medications to lessen some of the side effects of those potent drugs. Unfortunately the doctor soon found out that her mental state was delicately balanced around those drugs, and tampering with them could have dire consequences. During one of the times that they were tinkering with her meds, she came to us for an Easter visit. When the weather was good at Easter we would have an Easter egg hunt in our yard, which Bev always enjoyed. I would hide plastic eggs that contained candy and, of course, quarters. Bev was always enthusiastic about her searching, but this particular year it got a little out of hand. Since Jonnie's two girls were preteens at the time, they joined in on the hunt. Everyone had a basket and set about collecting eggs. Bev went barreling around the yard looking for eggs, as usual, but that year she wasn't satisfied with her own loot. Every time she saw one of the girls find an egg, she charged at her and grabbed the egg away to empty the contents into her own basket. Before long the girls dropped their baskets and ran into the house. Eventually Jonnie and I managed to calm Bev down and we took her back in as well. Today we laugh when we tell the girls how funny they looked running away from their aunt in their Easter finery, baskets flying, but, though we tried to make light of it, the incident had a more serious side. We certainly didn't want the girls to be afraid of their aunt and we didn't want Bev to be so agitated that she couldn't enjoy being with us. That meant that her medications needed to be adjusted yet again. Her doctors soon realized that they couldn't safely reduce the levels of her medications and that her mental well being depended on levels that were higher than what they would prefer to use.

For much of her life, Bev's story has been a sad one, and bright moments were few and far between. If there were any during her stay at Pennhurst, I don't know about them. I hope there were some. Honestly, though, I can't remember Bev smiling or laughing until after she left Pennhurst. By then she was forty four years old. Even photos taken of her when she was a little girl show a bewildered or melancholy expres-

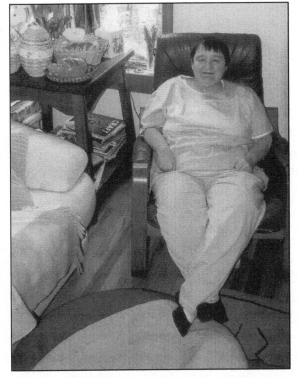

sion. Nowadays she has a wonderful toothless grin and smiles happily for the camera. She often giggles to herself, enjoying some private thought that tickles her. I sometimes feel that she finds us all highly amusing, that she knows some hilarious secret that she's not sharing.

Bev makes everyone around her smile. Everyone who meets her enjoys her company. She greets the world with a positive attitude, never complains, and has a great sense of humor. Part of her personality, however, is being obsessive/compulsive. One thing she became obsessed with is quarters. It began when she was employed in the Prospectus BERCO workshop on the production line, where she had regular breaks and lunchtime to look forward to. When it was time for a snack, she needed quarters for the vending machines, especially the soda machine which contained the soft drinks and iced tea she craved. As a result, she began hoarding quarters and begging friends, family, and total strangers for them. Her quest for quarters is legendary.

One day several years ago Jonnie and I visited Bev at her group home on her birthday. As a treat, we took her to dinner at a local restaurant. Bev loves food and enjoys going out to eat and choosing her own menu. For most of her adult life, Bev has had a weight issue, and, at the time of this particular outing, she was still quite heavy. Despite her weight, she could move very quickly and tended to be a bit of a "bull in a china shop". People who knew her were prepared to get out of her way, but people who were not could be caught off guard by her linebacker approach.

We had a pleasant dinner together, and the wait staff were especially attentive to Bev. Before we left the restaurant we took turns going to the restroom. I went first, then returned to the table and computed the tip while Jonnie and Bev went. After a few minutes I heard a ruckus going on out in the lobby. I had an ominous feeling about the noise and jumped up from the table to investigate. This restaurant was the type at which patrons paid their bills at a cash register on their way out. As Jonnie and Bev were coming out of the ladies room, they needed to walk right by the register. Unfortunately at that very moment a customer was getting her change after paying the bill and there were a couple of quarters lying on the counter. Before Jonnie could blink, Bev, nearly two hundred pounds of her, charged at the counter to scoop up the quarters, knocking down a waitress in the process. As soon as she realized what she had done, Bev began wailing "I'm sorry, I'm sorry!" I jumped in to help Jonnie comfort Bev, then pick up the waitress, and apologize profusely for the incident.

Luckily, no one was injured and everyone was very understanding about the whole event. Jonnie ushered Bev outside while I paid the bill and made sure everyone was okay. The waitress was wonderful. She got up and brushed herself off and insisted that we not make a fuss. I left a generous tip, no quarters, and went outside to join Bev and Jonnie in the parking lot. One look at each other and we burst out laughing. We couldn't help it. Bev, in her usual childlike fashion, forgot about it as soon as we were in the car, and we all went home and had birthday cake.

From then on, when we took Bev anywhere, we double teamed her and kept a sharp eye out for loose change!

Bev has always been a bundle of energy, and even though she has slowed down in the past few years, she still likes staying busy. When Bev first moved into her present group home she was working every day on a production line at Prospectus BERCO. She loved her job and still talks about going to the workshop even though she retired in 2002. This reminds me of our mother, who worked on a production line at Western Electric for over 25 years. They were both hard workers and did their best no matter what the task. Bev thrived on the workshop routine that keeping both her mind and hands busy, and she missed it when she retired. Once she stopped working, she began attending an adult day care program at an nearby facility which serves disabled and elderly clients. She and her housemates spend several hours there each day. The facility provides all sorts of activities like crafts, music, games, holiday and birthday celebrations, and live entertainment. In the quiet times Bev loves to do jigsaw puzzles and has become quite the puzzle wizard.

Years ago Bev used to go on all sorts of extended trips and excursions, and in the summer went away to camp, but now that she is older

and her health is more fragile, she stays closer to home. She gets tired more easily now, and with the dietary restrictions she needs, feeding her away from home can be difficult. In her younger days, though, she was always on the go. During the thirty plus years that she has lived in group homes she's had a lot of exciting experiences. As a matter of fact, she has travelled more and has seen more places than many people ever do. She has been on excursions to Disney World, Atlantic City, Baltimore Inner

Harbor, the Philadelphia Zoo, and to beaches in New Jersey and Delaware. She especially enjoyed Disney World and became a big fan of Mickey Mouse. The local trips she went on were escorted by Threshold staff, but for the longer trips she went with groups escorted by other providers who specialize in travel arrangements. In addition to her travels, for many years she also attended a week at a camp in the Poconos every summer. Another one of Bev's favorite activities, ever since she was a child, was going to amusement parks. She particularly liked going on the rides, especially the ferris wheel. There are two large amusement parks about an hour from Reading, and she has been to both of them many times. Besides her trips and outings, she also stayed physically active by going swimming and bowling every week. She has attended many supervised dances, parties, banquets, and other social activities sponsored by Threshold and other organizations, and she has always enjoyed shopping, eating out, and going to church, where she especially loves to sing. Even though her activities are more limited these days, she still has a busy and fulfilling life for someone her age.

It is thanks to Threshold, Prospectus BERCO, and Service Access Management that Bev has been afforded all of these opportunities. They say it takes a village to raise a child. It certainly is true for the children of Pennhurst. It takes a huge team of people to assure their welfare as they live out their lives in the wider world. All of the Pennhurst residents who were members of the class action lawsuit Halderman v. the Commonwealth of PA are guaranteed care for the rest of their lives. Court-approved guidelines for their care were set up, and advocates were appointed to make sure that they receive the services they are entitled to. In the beginning these advocates did an administrative job and didn't have contact with their charges unless a situation arose that required it. They monitored what went on in the group homes and other placements and they checked in with family members to make sure they were satisfied with how their relatives were being looked after. The advocates continue to perform that function, even though they still have well over seven hundred class action members to follow. The organizations and individuals responsible for the care of consumers in the program keep extensive records on each person and write endless reports. Twice a year they conduct an ISP, or Individual Support Plan, meeting with members of the team as well as concerned family members.

Ultimately, because of the class action suit, the Commonwealth of

Now

Pennsylvania is responsible for Bev's welfare for life. The biannual ISP meetings are the primary connection between the state appointed social service organizations and her family. Since the early 1990's I have been attending these meetings where we have discussed Bev's daily life, activities and trips, her work, and her health. By the time I became involved in her care she was fifty three years old and I found that I was just getting to know her. I knew more about her past than I knew about her present. Once I started going to those meetings I got to know the members of the team devoted to caring for her, and I began to appreciate the coordinated effort it took to support her. I learned about her complicated health history and her psychiatric diagnosis, her medications and her behavior modification plans. I became familiar with her living arrangements, her housemates, her daily schedule, and the people who were with her every minute of the day. I had no idea that so many people loved her and provided her with so much that her biological family did not.

It took the hard work of many dedicated staff to bring Bev and others like her into the outside world and give them a full and productive life. Writing Bev's story has opened my eyes to what they have accomplished. When I look back and see how far Bev has come since she walked out the doors of Pennhurst in 1983, I am overwhelmed. Her transformation has been nothing short of a miracle. My only regret is that we had so little to do with it. When she left Pennhurst, we did not rally around and welcome her back into the bosom of the family. Of course, we never were very good at rallying. We saw her a little more often, but we were still primarily just visitors. Even after she began living in group homes, we never spent more than a few hours at a time with her. She never stayed overnight in any of our homes. Her day to day life centered around her housemates and the Threshold staff, not with us. Through the years that I've been working with them, I have admired their commitment to providing a safe, loving and happy environment for her. I am ever grateful to all the people who not only do their jobs, but also take her into their lives and hearts.

These days the familiar faces in Bev's family group belong to me, Jonnie and her girls Hannah and Mary, and my husband Greg. These are the faces she sees when she comes to my house for her home visits. However, even though she knows us all well, she reacts differently to us when we are in our home than when we see her elsewhere. The tables are turned when we are the visitors in her group home or day care center. She continues to keep her two worlds separate, just as she always has. When she does come home with us, I often get the feeling that she is expecting my house to somehow morph into her cherished childhood home, that she is waiting for our younger selves to run in the door and play with her, and that Mom and Dad will appear from the next room at any moment. When we look at her today we can see our parents' faces reflected in hers and all the memories become real for us too. It is that link that truly makes us family, even though we are not with her every day.

Bev's life in her group home is wonderful and she is well looked after, but it is sad that since the age of nine she has not been able to live with any of us. She went from a miserable institutional life at Pennhurst to a much happier life, but she never really went home again and never will. On June 11, 1952 she left her family forever. Each day, from that day forward, took her further and further away from everything and everyone she so desperately needed. Despite the best efforts of the Commonwealth of Pennsylvania, and all the wonderful people who have stood by her since she walked out of Pennhurst in 1983, no one can ever make up for what she lost. No one can ever make up for what we lost.

Now that Greg and Jonnie and I are all older, Bev has slipped into a comfortable niche in our lives. Our families have all grown through the years and, as they did, Bev became part of expanded group.

Fortunately, the three of us were all blessed with spouses who embraced Bev as part of the family and who were always good and kind to her. They each developed their own relationship with her and taught their children about special people like Bev in the process as well.

Greg's wife Chris, the first addition to our extended family, got to know Bev not long after they were married. In the early seventies she went to Pennhurst to visit Bev with various members of our family, taking gifts and birthday cakes and orchestrating the proceedings. At other times, Dad would pick Bev up at Pennhurst and take her to Greg and Chris's home, a quaint country farmhouse where they lived with their three young children, Lesley, Andrea, and Bryan. Chris would entertain her there, providing Bev with the comforting experiences that meant so much to her. She is a very nurturing person who always did her best to make Bev feel loved and cared for. Unfortunately, Chris's involvement with Bev ended when Greg moved the family, including their new baby son, to Brazil in 1978 to pursue a long career as a missionary in South America. Greg and Chris never lived anywhere near Bev again and had very few opportunities to see her. As for their children, they were introduced to their Aunt Bev while she was still living at Pennhurst and had not yet bloomed into the more complete person she would later become. The youngest, Jeremy, never got to know her at all. At the time that Bev moved into her group home to start her new life, they were still in Brazil, and later were scattered across the United States living their own adult lives. They haven't seen her since before they left for Brazil and have limited memories of her from their childhood.

My husband Greg, the next spouse to join our ranks, has a long history with Bev, starting with visits to see her at Pennhurst even before we were married. He was with us in the early 1970's when we went to Pennhurst to visit as a family, and he went along with Dad and me to see Bev's new living quarters when she moved to a different building on campus. Through the years he has grown to know Bev very well and has always gotten along comfortably with both her and her housemates and friends. After my parents passed away, he and I took over the responsibility of arranging her visits and transporting her to and from her group home. We've had many car rides with Bev singing the oldies along with the radio or belting out Christmas carols with somewhat altered lyrics. Over ten years ago he began attending the individual support plan meetings with me and has gotten to know the Threshold staff well, not only at Threshold meetings, but also at quite a few of Bev's medical appointments. Besides his many trips to both her group home and her adult day care facility, he has driven countless miles transporting Bev for her visits with our family. When it came time to do research for this book, he took me to the Norristown State Hospital where I could examine Bev's Pennhurst records and waited patiently while I pored over the musty files. He has always been totally supportive of all our efforts to care for Bev. As far as Bev is concerned, he is as much a fixture in the family picture by now as any of the rest of us.

By the time Jonnie's husband, Dave, became part of the family, Bev's Pennhurst days were already behind her. He was fortunate to get to know her in a family setting instead of the institution. When Jonnie was married to Dave, he came along to both Mother's and Dad's house to see Bev when they had her for visits. The most memorable were the

Easter luncheons with all of us tightly tucked around the table in Mother's small dining room in her apartment. After our parents both passed away, we often brought Bev to Jonnie and Dave's house for visits, especially at Christmastime. Their family lived in a modern house on top of a mountain near a local ski complex. It was a lively home full of hustle and bustle and fun. They had two daughters together, Hannah and Mary, and one girl, Amy, from Dave's previous marriage. Dave enjoyed those family gatherings and happily included Bev in the festivities. Hannah, Mary, and Amy grew up knowing Bev as an essential member of the family and got to know their Aunt Bev quite well. Later, in her college years, Amy often drove Bev back to her group home after holiday celebrations. Dave himself also took many turns doing the driving to return Bev to her house at the end of the day. He was never anything but kind and welcoming to Bev in his home, and she had many happy times with all of us there. As for the girls, though Bev is not part of Amy's life any more, Hannah and Mary have continued to see her through the years at holiday celebrations at my house. Just recently, though, all three of them joined in the celebration of Bev's seventieth birthday at a special party. Their own loving relationship with each other as sisters helps them appreciate how important Bev is to Jonnie and me.

Both my brother Greg and sister Jonnie have children, but I do not. I admire them for the bravery and optimism that they showed in having them. Greg and Chris raised two girls and two boys, one adopted as a preteen. To add to the challenge they packed all four of them up and took them to Brazil where they became missionary kids. Jonnie and Dave raised two lovely girls in more conventional circumstances in Pennsylvania. When I was a little girl playing house with my friends, I pretended I was the mother to a house full of children. At that time, it seemed like a wonderful idea. But later, in my teens, when the prospect of marriage and children became more than a game, fear guided me in another direction. After years of seeing my mother struggle with having a mentally handicapped child, I decided that I could never face that kind of challenge. Being responsible for healthy children was daunting enough, but to have the strength to raise a handicapped child was out of the question. Even if I were lucky enough to have a healthy child, I felt inadequate to raise her to be a happy person. I pictured her as a copy of myself. I imagined her lying awake in her bed at night, gripped by a nameless fear, or crying herself to sleep in the dark. I believed I could not be a fit mother for anyone, that I should never have children. Later in my life, after going through psychotherapy, I finally felt ready for a child emotionally, but by then I was in my late thirties and I wasn't physically able to be a mom. After years of infertility treatments and a miscarriage, I had to except the fact that I had missed my chance.

My years of psychotherapy were a lifesaver for me. Though I had suppressed the fears that haunted me through grade school, through high school, and even into my college years, they eventually manifested themselves in continual anxiety and crippling panic attacks that became overpowering by the time I reached my late twenties. Though I coped brilliantly, I finally reached the breaking point and was forced to do something to change the fractured pattern of my life. After suffering with agoraphobia and panic attacks, and letting them control my life well into my thirties, I made the decision to enter into psychotherapy. It was only after going through that process that I was able to overcome the severe anxiety disorder that had been developing since my teens. After years of hard work, both with the therapist and on my own, I was able to free myself of so many demons and live my life without persistent fear.

One of the most important things that a person takes away from therapy is the ability to analyze her life, past and present, and work it through on her own. Therapy done right is an ongoing process that never ends, even after the office visits stop. My therapy helped me close the door on old fears and worries and open a new one that led to a better life. Eventually I came to write this book, to tell this story not to a therapist, but to the printed page, and to finally shed light on a shadowy corner of my life that for so long lay hidden from the world and forgotten by myself. It wasn't until our parents passed away and I began to take over their role in Bev's life that I was able to face the truth about what Bev really meant to me and how intertwined our lives had always been. With that understanding another layer of fear melted away.

When I am with Bev these days I feel a kind of peace. I see how she has gone on to live a contented life after the chaos and strife of her earlier days. She has accepted what has happened and, though she surely carries some frightful memories with her, she lives in the moment. She bears the scars, both visible and invisible, of what went before, but she wears them with the innocence of a child. Here and now is all that matters. She is unfailingly cheerful no matter what she has to endure. She is a walking lesson in life who tells me in her own way to let go of the past. There is nothing to fear anymore.

~19~

Forever and Ever, Amen

When we look at people like Bev we see what's inside. It's like looking at someone with a ghastly wound that reveals what's under our own skin. We don't want to see it. It disturbs us to know that we are looking at what is inside ourselves, exposed instead of safely under cover. What we see in their behavior is what we all would be without the subterfuge we use to conduct our lives in a socially acceptable fashion. They are us without rules, and we do not want to look. We do not want to know what lies within us all. We do not want to admit that they are us.

We are a society obsessed with looking good. We like to see attractive people, well groomed and well dressed. We generally pay more attention to how we look than how we feel. There was a character on the TV show Saturday Night Live years ago named Fernando who said repeatedly, "It is better to look good than to feel good." Most of us act as though that were true. Far more people will spend time and money on fashion consultants, personal trainers, or plastic surgeons than on psychologists, counselors, or other mental health professionals. It is so very important to look good, and intellectually handicapped people generally do not look good. The mental impairment that disturbs their minds often shows in their faces, in their stances, and in their gaits. Their eyes may not quite focus, their speech can be slurred or distorted, their words unintelligible or inappropriate, their facial expressions might be vacant or in constant motion. They may make odd noises, be loud or boisterous. They may move with uncoordinated or aggressive movements. They may often look strange and act strange. They can make "normal" people feel uncomfortable or wary. No wonder most people want them out of sight. They don't want to be reminded about how mysterious our minds are, about how easy it is for the brain to be injured, how thin the line is between the normal and abnormal, sanity and madness.

Obviously my siblings and I feel perfectly comfortable when we are with our sister Bev. Quite frankly I forget that most people never have any occasion to interact with intellectually disabled people. Since only 2 to 3 percent of the population is classified as intellectually disabled, they are easily overlooked. Even though I have said that Bev sometimes seemed like a stranger in our family, by the same token it has always been so natural to be with her. In a way, having her as our sister has been a rare gift. It has made us all live differently, has given us all a unique view of the world. For one thing, we all have a grand sense of humor. Like Bev, we find humor where others might not. Irony is everywhere. It has also made us better people than we otherwise might have been. We are empathetic. We know suffering when we see it. We treasure life, despite its hardships. In truth, Bev is our touchstone.

When we gather for family meals at holidays, we almost always give Bev the honor of saying the blessing. She recites the Lord's Prayer for us in her own special way. She repeats it perfectly as far as "give us this day our daily bread", but for some reason from that point on she ad libs whatever is on her mind until she finally ends with "forever and ever, amen." Of course, what is on her mind is usually food. Her most memorable line, one that cracked us all up, was "give us this day our daily bread and please send cheese." Her childlike innocence is a reminder to all of us to not take ourselves, or anything else, too seriously. She has distilled life down to its very basic components. When you are with her there is nothing but the here and now. Tomorrow does not exist and the past is just a dream. She is cheerful and funny and brave. We could all take a page from her book when it comes to learning how to live.

I admire my sister Beverley. With her baby soft skin and toothless smile, she inspires me. She has been through so much in her life, things most of us can't even imagine. The stories she could tell would curl your hair. Yet, despite all that she has endured, from her unfair start in life to years of incarceration, isolation, neglect, and overmedication, she held on to a spark that has never failed. In her own special way, she has passed it on.

That spark will never die.

~20~

Legacy

Pennhurst State School and Hospital is long gone, but its empty, decaying buildings still stand in the middle of the Pennsylvania countryside, silent testimony to decades of human suffering. Ever since Pennhurst was closed in 1987, there has been controversy about what to do with this sprawling property and the debate is ongoing. According to state policy the disposition of the property is under the control of the Department of General Services. Shortly after taking possession of Pennhurst the Department transferred about 144 acres to the Department of Military Affairs which maintains the Southeastern Pennsylvania Veterans' Center on the site. A National Guard armory is also housed in one of the buildings on the upper campus. Some of the land is used for farming, and some small parcels were sold to private concerns, including the Philadelphia Electric Company. A huge parcel is now the Spring Hollow Golf Club, which uses one of the old dairy barns as part of its elaborate clubhouse. Most of the original campus, however, continues to deteriorate as it sits year after year with very little care or maintenance.

Over the years the stately Jacobean Revival buildings have been vandalized by scavengers looking for copper and other valuable materials which could be sold for a profit, or by thrill seekers who came to explore their cavernous interiors and leave graffiti behind to commemorate their visits. Some people claim the structures are haunted and believe they see ghosts and hear screaming in the night. Television programs about the paranormal have been filmed here with hyped up hosts searching in the dark for evidence of tormented spirits. In 2010 an annual "Haunted Asylum" attraction was opened on the property to amuse people looking for a Halloween fright. The abandoned buildings do evoke an eerie sense of melancholy, with their dilapidated condition making the air of despair almost palpable. It is a place that can give you goosebumps. For those of us whose family members once lived there, it is a place that can bring you to tears.

The Pennhurst site is currently mired in seemingly endless legal and financial wrangling. In 2008 the property was sold for two million dollars to private developers who have bought other state hospital properties and turned them into commercial enterprises. Historic preservation is not their primary concern. To  advocate for a meaningful and respectful use of the site, the Pennhurst Memorial and Preservation Alliance formed in 2008 and applied to have the campus added to the National Register of Historic Places. In January 2009 Pennhurst, through PM&PA, became a member of the International Coalition of Sites of Conscience, a worldwide network of historic sites specifically dedicated to remembering struggles for justice. The PM&PA wants the site to house a museum, research center, and conference facility to preserve Pennhurst's place in history and to educate the public about the continuing struggle of people with disabilities. Recently a five-year plan was put in place to use the former superintendent's house as a museum and interpretive center. Their website eloquently states their goal:

> We seek to reclaim this once painful place as a center of conscience, healing, and outreach. This process is essential in the creation and preservation of a society where, all people are val-

ued and respected, and where all people have the knowledge, opportunity, and power to improve their lives and the lives of others.

It remains to be seen what will eventually happen to the place that was Pennhurst. The fight goes on. For those whose loved ones lived and sometimes died there, it is a symbol of their struggle to survive in a world that did not welcome them. This is not a place that should be turned into a shopping mall or office space or luxury apartments that erase the past. Some part of it needs to be preserved as an ever present reminder of what happened there. We owe that, at least, to the people whose lives were lived within its walls. This has been the story of my sister Bev, just one story out of thousands. Those thousands of stories need to be told, need to be preserved, need to be honored. We must never forget them.

EPILOGUE

Our beloved sister Beverley passed away suddenly not long before the publication of this book. It happened on Sunday, February 8, 2015. I got a phone call at around 1:00 in the afternoon from a doctor at the Reading Hospital emergency room. "How soon can you get here?" she asked. "Bring your other sister if you can." By 3:00 Jonnie and I were by Bev's bedside, watching her struggle to breathe through a respirator. At 6:00 that evening we held her hands and said "good bye".

I wanted so much to place this book in her hands, to hold a joyous book signing, and have her autograph it. Instead it will have to stand as her memoriam, a tribute to a life bravely lived. I couldn't bring myself to go back and rewrite it in the past tense. I left it the way it is. In it, she is alive, and always will be. Although her loss was a painful shock, it added yet another amazing chapter to her story, and to the lessons she has taught me along the way. Her memorial service, held five weeks after her passing, was perhaps the most poignant of all.

The service was attended by her family of siblings and their partners, nieces, friends, and Threshold staff and residents. If anyone doubts for one minute the contribution to life that intellectually challenged people like Bev have to give, they should have been there that day. The love, the heartfelt praise and admiration, the tears shed by all of us, were a testimony to her place in the world. I have been to many funerals and memorials through the years, and none has been more sincerely touching than hers. She was loved, she was valued, she was cherished by everyone who knew her. We should all be so lucky.

NON FINITUR

29820253R00137

Made in the USA
Middletown, DE
03 March 2016